BRILLIANCE

An 'other' woman's history

Contents

INTRODUCTION

"Throughout history people have knocked their heads against the riddle of the nature of femininity... Nor will you have escaped worrying over this problem – those of you who are men; to those of you who are women this will not apply – you are yourselves the problem." [1]

Sigmund Freud

In 2019, a Forbes article citing the top 100 most innovative leaders in the United States listed one woman amongst 99 men.[2] One.

Sadly, that is probably not all that surprising to you. But how surprised would you be if I told you that brilliance – the kind of brilliance required to be successful, to lead others, to create things, to make a difference in the world, the kind of brilliance that others aspire to – was a boy thing? Well, spoiler alert... it's not. I'm willing to bet there is a large part of you that already knew that. I'm also willing to bet there's a smaller part of you that understands that this is 'the way it is' but perhaps can't put your finger on why. The fact that only one woman made Forbes's list points in big shiny neon lights to an issue we desperately need to address – society does not see women as equally brilliant or capable as men. In fact, men's capability is assumed, women's on the other hand, must be proved. And the really sad thing? Girls are growing up believing this to be true. And that belief, or should I say that *myth*, starts early. Like really early.

Two years before that Forbes article, a study was conducted to understand when gender stereotypes about intellectual ability start to form. Researchers asked children to assign traits like 'being smart' to pictures of women and men.[3] The results were depressing. At age five, both girls and boys were just as likely to associate brilliance with their own gender. However, just one year later, at age six, that perception had changed. More boys chose their own gender as 'really, really smart' whilst fewer girls were choosing theirs.[4] Girls had started to believe that being really smart was a boy thing.

Reading that study made me sad. Then it made me angry. It made me question; what on earth is happening to make six-year-olds believe that? What had I grown up believing brilliance looked like? What had shaped my image of successful women? Now, a deep dive into your own beliefs, choices, and expectations is not always the most comfortable. And I'll admit, what I came back to the surface with surprised me. I liked to think of myself as an empowered woman, wise to the stereotypes and biases that we deal with on a daily basis, confident in my personal aspirations. Surely, I hadn't succumbed to the social editing women and girls faced? The beauty ads making us think that smooth skin is the most important thing in the world, social media touting the new wedding must-haves or latest diet hack, the high street shops helping you dress for the role you want. My thoughts landed on when I'd turned 30. I have to say, I didn't mind turning 30. I'd been fortunate enough to enjoy and achieve a lot of the things I'd really wanted to – I'd graduated from university and started a career. I'd travelled the world and met some incredible people. I had a supportive and fun group of friends, a roof over my head, and my own transport. All in all, I had a very happy, privileged life. However, on turning 30 there was a teeny, tiny part of me that felt like I'd failed. That nagging feeling of failure, I realised, came down to a few things that hadn't materialised. I had attached various (and seemingly) arbitrary milestones to my life. Milestones that I'd expected to hit and absolutely hadn't. Buy a house at 25, married at 26, kids at 29. But these milestones weren't arbitrary. They were stereotypes I'd learnt to believe marked women's success. I had been measuring myself against someone else's yard stick.

Sitting here now, almost 10 years later, I'm a big believer that success is intensely personal and looks different for everyone. After a decade more life experience, learning, and doing a *lot* of inner work, I'm very clear on what success means to me: feeling comfortable with who I am, having my voice heard and respected, a fulfilling career using my coaching expertise to support other women to succeed, having loving friends and family, financial freedom, and some adventure sprinkled here and there. But what does that actually *look* like? Well, I guess it looks like the freedom to choose where I spend my time and who I spend it with. It looks like asserting my personal boundaries to support my wellbeing. It looks like being clear on my career aspirations and making choices that align with them. It looks like speaking up when I have something to say and those in the room listening and taking note. It looks like eating healthily *and* not feeling guilty about having a pizza if I fancy it. It looks like acknowledging my changing body and appreciating what it has helped me achieve. It looks like celebrating wins – big or small – like achieving a qualification, leaving a toxic job or relationship, or completing a Tough Mudder.

Now you will all have your own thoughts on what success looks like of course. As a white woman living in the UK, I am keenly aware that my perspective and experience is exactly that – *my* perspective and experience. Speaking about women as a group is always challenging and it is important to acknowledge that neither our experiences nor our fight for equality are equal – being a woman intersects with many other characteristics that have their own battles for equality being fought. I'm incredibly conscious that what this book is addressing is a small facet of women's identity, in that being a woman is just one part. Most of us are women AND. And our race. And our sexual orientation. And our religion. And our nationality. And our social class. I do believe though that for all of us, being a woman means fighting a constant battle against forces trying to limit our freedoms, potential, and presence.

Whilst researching and writing this book I have come to realise that my personal success measures are *not* the things by which society measures my success as a woman. Contemplating what success looks like for yourself takes time, it takes work. It's much easier and faster to follow what we see around us. Human beings are after all social animals, and we have an evolutionary need to fit into the group.

So, forget my thoughts for a moment. What does society require of successful women? If you look hard enough today, you will find society's expectations and regulations imposed on women everywhere. From glossy magazine covers telling us how to dress, to unspoken rules on how we should communicate (and in case you're in any doubt that means being 'nice' at all times). From abortion laws which restrict our bodily freedoms, to titles like Miss or Mrs which denote our availability. From clothing emblazoned with instructions like 'keep smiling', to suggestions that women with power should be feared (this one was wonderfully demonstrated by Donald Trump's 2016 presidential campaign which sold t-shirts and tote bags emblazoned with images of Trump as Perseus holding up the severed Medusa-esque head of Hillary Clinton). The list goes on. And once you start noticing these things, it's hard to stop. For instance, when I started looking (I mean *really* looking) I noticed that the representation of women in the media was so different to men that it impacted how people saw our accomplishments and credibility. I noticed that social constructs influenced our expectations of ourselves as women and the expectations others have of us too. I noticed that women and men view failure differently because men are born into a society made in their image, and women are not. I even learned that being a woman could increase your chances of dying in a disaster. Most of all, I realised that all these things had subconsciously influenced my own choices, behaviours, and expectations.

Society denotes successful women as thin, white, and pretty. They smile and are *always* likeable. They don't talk too loud or take up too much space. Successful women are the ultimate carers, they are wives and mothers before anything else. They're demure but not dowdy, sexy but not slutty, empowered but not powerful. They're allowed to compete but not to complain, even though the system is rigged. Women are a square peg in a round hole, just waiting to have our corners sanded down so we can fit our awkward bodies and our different needs into a world geared towards the generic male. We are the 'other', the second sex.

I should clarify from the outset that this book is not intended to be a 'down with men' piece of propaganda – far from it. I believe that *everyone* has value and insight to offer our world. However, a patriarchal society – one in which men hold the power – like so many of us live in does not allow that to happen equally or easily. Patriarchy is a social system that affects both women *and* men negatively. It's the reason men feel the need to be macho and struggle to talk about their mental health; it's also the reason women are seen as life's carers and win custody battles more often. However, the very nature of this book means I'm focusing on how society and this system impacts women specifically. Many, if not all, of the biases, stereotypes, and behaviours we'll come across in the following pages are perpetuated by both men and women – after all, we are a product of the societies and cultures we were raised and live in. And given that society has largely been built for and around men, it's unsurprising that these serve to limit women's brilliance.

So why is this the way it is? Why are women's expectations of life, career paths, domestic responsibilities, and place in society still clouded by inequality? How have we arrived at a point where even in the 21st century girls grow up believing that these unattainable standards are what is required of ordinary women and that brilliance belongs to the boys? To answer these questions, we have to go back to the beginning. We have to understand how the story of women has unfolded.

Because if we want to change the narrative, we need to take ownership of the story. As luck would have it, diving back into history to come up with answers is right up my street. I've always been fascinated by what came before: ancient societies glittering with gold and incredible architecture, customs and cultures so vastly different from my own, stories and legends about heroes and monsters. I've always loved it. Still do. So much so in fact that I spent three years at university studying it. Over the course of this book, I will take you on a tour through the millennia. I will tell women's story, our story, in as much depth and colour as I'm able. Together, we will explore how women have been shaped by history and by the societies we live in. We'll uncover where the stereotypes and falsehoods come from, and how over years they have become accepted as fact. And by the end it is my hope that you won't just believe, but you will *know* that women are brilliant. You will feel empowered to set your own measures of success, and you will no longer accept a world that tries to sand down your corners.

So here we are, at the beginning of a journey to deconstruct the myth, meet it head on, stare it in the face, and correct the idea that brilliance is a boy thing. Because it isn't.

A Stroll Through History

"History isn't what happened. It's who tells the story."

Sally Rorschach Wagner

One of the first written assignments given to me as a young fresher at university was to complete a short essay answering the question "why study history?". I remember coming away from that first lecture thinking what a breeze that homework would be and that I could scribble out a quick answer and make my merry way to the pub. The reality though was that was a far harder question to answer than I'd appreciated.

The past is so tightly woven into our present that sometimes – a lot of the time – we can't even see it. It just, is. Think about it, have you ever questioned why women are branded 'emotional'? Or why women seem to walk an infinite line between perfection and failure? Understanding our past helps us make meaning of our present. It gives us context. It allows us to learn from experience and, crucially, it equips us to make different choices about our future.

Back then I thought of history as fact, which in theory it is. However, I quickly learned that just like we see today, historical events were narrated with the storyteller's own motivations, values, and biases aplenty. *History isn't what happened. It's who tells the story*. How often do we see the same global event served up to us differently according to which newspaper we're reading or news channel we're watching? People's opinions and perspectives inevitably influence how they view events and therefore how they retell the story. History is no different. It has largely been written by those in charge, and for the majority of human history that has been men. The result of this is twofold. Firstly, we are painted a picture of the past through a male lens leaving us with a somewhat skewed view of events, society, and life within it. The societal values, stereotypes, and stories that made it into the history books are the ones that have prevailed and now influence our own lives. Secondly, it means that the ordinary woman in the historical record can be pretty difficult to find given that male efforts and accomplishments were considered far more noteworthy.

Our experience of being a woman today has been moulded by millennia of these values, stereotypes, and stories – many of which were designed to exert control, to bury women's voices, to undermine their credibility, and demonstrate what is and is not 'acceptable'. Piecing together the scattered evidence we do have, we find a story unfolding about how women became a second citizen. From the very first cities there is evidence across the globe of ideals, standards, even laws, which prevented women from contributing to society in the same way as men. Should a woman get beyond herself, she would be either consigned to anonymity or villainy. Those that managed to reach the lofty heights of power and infamy could expect their reputations muddied and names obliterated. The air of mystery that has long been constructed around women has become a convenient excuse for patriarchal societies to ignore or sideline anything that feels different, difficult, or confusing.

Whilst researching this book I found that women have, on the whole, been operating under a different set of expectations to men. We've been valued differently and judged more heavily for centuries. But encouragingly, I also found that this isn't an inevitability. There are civilisations and societies that didn't 'other' their women. And in the ones that did, there are examples of women who broke the mould and let their brilliance shine through.

THE WRONG END OF THE STICK

Some years ago, I was attending a leadership coaching conference. Having left university with a degree in Ancient History & Archaeology, I made the move into – you guessed it – the hospitality sector. Admittedly not a move I'd bargained for, but it brought me to my other passion and current work – career coaching. The conference was the usual setup. Anyone who has ever attended events like this will attest that many of them blend into one another: a seamless stream of tea and coffee, presentations, group discussions, and the odd role play that everyone is internally cringing at. Occasionally, however, some of them leave their mark. It might be an inspirational story, a motivational quote, or in my case the answer to a question: "Want to know the depressing truth about the brain?". The guest speaker had my attention. The answer was every bit as depressing as the question promised. *Facts don't matter*. Not if they don't align with what we already believe to be true. It turns out that as human beings we have an inbuilt tendency to embrace the stuff that supports our beliefs and discard the stuff that doesn't. It's hardwired. Our brains love consistency and, incredibly, when faced with facts that do not stack up with our strongly held beliefs; our education, scientific evidence, data, and even our ability to reason goes right out the window.[5]

This depressing truth popped back into my head when I stumbled across a National Geographic article one night whilst doom-scrolling social media. In 2018, a team of archaeologists working on a dig site in Peru discovered the burial of a single adult alongside an extensive kit of stone hunting tools dating back 9000 years. Scattered around the burial were projectiles for taking down large mammals, rocks for cracking bones and preparing hides, and sharp stone flakes for chopping meat. On uncovering this impressive find, the team's immediate assumption was that he must have been, not only an accomplished hunter, but a very important person within the society he came from.[6] *He*.

When the bones were analysed, it became apparent that what they had found was actually a biological female – and it appears that this isn't an anomaly. Today, women in the workplace are frequently robbed of the credit for their work. It turns out we may have been doing this to women who existed thousands of years ago too. Picture a hunter-gatherer society for a second. What immediately comes to mind? Maybe men with spears tracking a woolly mammoth whilst women and children pick berries nearby? Well, if so, you're not alone. Common assumption has designated women the gatherers and men the hunters. This is most likely down to a mix of modern studies of hunter-gatherer societies and current beliefs about gender roles.

But recent evidence suggests we may have spent decades with the wrong end of the stick. When previously studied hunter burials of a similar age in the Americas were looked at again, it became clear that up to half of them could have been female instead of male as previously assumed. And there was more evidence lying in plain sight – fossil evidence even suggested that males and females had the same hunting injuries. It's all in how the data is interpreted. Here we have a perfect example of a conflict between beliefs and evidence. The discovery of the female hunter raised questions – could we be sure this individual was a hunter in life? Did the tools even belong to them? It's only when the evidence challenges our existing beliefs that questions like this arise. Had the skeleton been male, it's unlikely they'd ever even be asked. This gives us a glimpse into just how easy it is to get carried away with incorrect assumptions, to create a narrative around gender and roll it out to the masses – just like the idea that boys are really smart, and girls are not. Depressing, huh?

So, what else might this hardwiring have misled us on? Alongside the discovery that prehistoric men and women were likely both hunters comes evidence to challenge long-held assumptions about the creators of cave art. We've all seen images of those early paintings: bison, woolly mammoths, reindeer, horses – all etched in charcoal, and the silhouettes of human hands in red ochre – hands that touched those cave walls tens of thousands of years ago, and yet their imprint remains. You can imagine how the animal figures might seem to dance out of the darkness when lit up by a small fire, heads appearing to bob, legs appearing to move. Amongst the animals and the handprints, images of goddess-like figures of naked women are also carved into the rock. A significant feature of Palaeolithic cave art, figures like the *Venus of Laussel* are thought to represent fertility. Painted in the colour of life, blood red, the *Venus of Laussel* is a nude woman carved into the limestone of a rock shelter in the Dordogne area of south-west France. With one hand on her large belly, in the other she holds a crescent shaped object marked with thirteen lines. Interpretations differ on what the crescent might represent – with thirteen lines it may relate to the lunar cycle and therefore combined with her large, perhaps pregnant, belly it may represent fertility. Or maybe she is holding a bison horn as a symbol of the hunt and with the other carvings at Laussel she represents a goddess assisting the hunter. Either way, her mystery continues to make her a magical figure and reminds us that cave art goes beyond stick men with spears.

Debates continue to rage amongst archaeologists and researchers about why these paintings exist. Some theories suggest that they were created by male hunters trying to weave a kind of magic to ensure a bountiful hunt or that they represent a visual story chronicling their kills. Others suppose that these are the work of shamans who had wandered deep into the womb-like caves to conduct rituals and recreated the visions they experienced whilst in a spiritual trance. Others simply believe that it was art for art's sake. Whatever the real reason behind these images, one thing upon which scholars agreed – they were made by men. That is until an archaeologist called Dean Snow began a piece of research on handprints found in eight cave sites across France and Spain. Analysis of these handprints – specifically looking at relative lengths of certain fingers –

concluded that 75 percent of them were female.[7] Women created most of our oldest-known cave art. Women were the first storytellers. Women left the marks that give us our clearest connection with our ancestors.

Inevitably this incredible piece of research raises more questions than perhaps it answers. In an article titled "Were the First Artists Mostly Women?" Snow admits the question he gets asked most often is why these ancient artists left their handprints at all. His response? "I have no idea, but a pretty good hypothesis is that this is somebody saying, 'This is mine, I did this,'".[8] I love that. Like a modern-day artist signing their canvas these people, whoever they were, left their mark – a mark that reaches through millennia – quite literally on their work.

For decades scholars and scientists have made unwarranted assumptions about the division of labour in pre-historic life, and it has dominated our understanding of women's role. We will of course never know for sure, but this new research indicates that women were far from a sideshow and instead were hunting big game and creating artwork to tell their stories, connect with the spiritual, or bring about the magical. They were integral to daily life.

Almost every civilisation has set limits on women's freedom, movement, and speech. But women's inequality hasn't always been the case. Around 9000 years ago, humans began to make a change from a nomadic way of life to one that was settled; the very beginnings of urban living and society as we know it. In modern day Turkey lies an archaeological site called Catalhoyuk that captures this exact moment in our history.

Regarded as the most significant human settlement documenting early settled life, it was an egalitarian society – one based on the principle that all people are equal, with equal rights and opportunities, rather than the patriarchal model we're used to.[9] This more equal way of living shows up in skeletons from the site and demonstrates males and females had similar experiences in both life and death, with the same housing, diet, time spent outdoors, and burials.[10] Now that whole family groups were settled in one place alongside others, the fertility of the land became increasingly important as people relied on it to provide enough food for everyone. And like the *Venus of Laussel*, the connection between fertility and the life-giving abilities of the female body can be found here at the very beginnings of society. This representation of fertility takes the form of clay figurines, one such sculpture being *The Seated Woman of Catalhoyuk* – a nude woman seated on a throne. This beautiful woman with her pendulous breasts and powerful pose is thought to be a Mother Goddess figure in the process of giving birth. However, more recent theories suggest she represents older women who have risen to achieve prominence and status in their community. The jury is still out on whether these figurines were the objects of worship, but clearly the power of the female was celebrated and respected by the people of Catalhoyuk. This was a place where gender equality flourished and undoes any notion that societies modelled on patriarchy are simply the natural order of things.[11] Our discoveries about women's roles as hunters, as artists, as creators and life-givers show that women were an equal part of prehistory, yet assumptions and those telling the story have rendered us mislabelled and left out. From these equal beginnings, the rise of the modern city was about to change everything.

THE RISE OF PATRIARCHY

If our discoveries about prehistory are right, and males and females had a far more equal role to play in societal groups than we've been led to believe, then there must have come a point where roles diverged, expectations changed, and men and women took up different places in society. The next part of our story takes us to ancient Mesopotamia, a geographical region that is now modern-day Iraq, where we see the emergence of cities and the very beginnings of this shift. As people began to master the art of agriculture there became less and less need to migrate around the land searching for vital resources. Stable food supplies meant that populations exploded far beyond small family groups and city-like civilisations began to develop.

With less time needed to source food, people's attention could now be focused elsewhere. It seems obvious really. When the important stuff is taken care of, there's suddenly much more space for other things, things like thinking and creating.

Not too long ago I dropped my son off for his first day of nursery. It was an emotional day leaving him for the first time. Prior to that my days had been spent with him at the park playing on the swings, reading *Fox's Socks* over and over again, and playing with every toy for approximately three seconds before leaving it in favour of the next one. Mealtimes took so long that by the time one ended it was almost time for the next. Getting anything done beyond the basics of childcare was quite frankly miraculous. I felt pretty accomplished if I'd managed to get one load of washing done. That day though, that first day without him, time seemed to stretch on endlessly. My intention had been to have a rare day of rest and relaxation. But by the time I picked him up from nursery, I had taken myself on a long walk, vacuumed the house, and for the first time in 10 months picked up the manuscript of this book and begun writing again. I had created something. And instead of ending the day feeling tired and like I'd achieved very little, I felt energised and inspired.

Now, you might be familiar with Maslow's Hierarchy of Needs, the theory (often shown as a pyramid) that as human beings we strive to meet our most basic needs first – those critical to our survival such as food, water, and shelter. Once these have been achieved, Maslow suggests that we seek to achieve higher and higher levels of need moving up the pyramid until we reach 'self-actualisation', meaning all that we are capable of being. These levels of need are often represented as follows:

5. Self-Actualisation
4. Self-Esteem
3. Love, belonging
2. Safety, security
1. Physiology, body

Maslow believed that the higher-level needs could only be addressed once the lower-level needs had at least been partly satisfied.[12] This theory puts the emergence of the city-state into context. It makes absolute sense then that once our ancestors had established the basics of a stable food supply and permanent shelter, they were able to shift their attention to higher needs like safety, security, or belonging. It is perhaps because of this that Mesopotamia gave us many of the greatest inventions in human history: writing, the wheel, mathematics, and the first irrigation systems. And as such is regarded as one of the first great civilisations. However, along with what we recognise as the foundations of society as we know it, Mesopotamia also gave us some of the earliest written law codes and with those, the relegation of women to the second-class citizen.

As much as I would love to walk you through all of it, Mesopotamian history is long and complex involving multiple empires and kings that ruled over the region. I can't do it justice here, nor do I need to for our purposes. However, if we examine it closely, we can see within it the moments when women's freedoms began to change in contrast to what we saw at Catalhoyuk.

Early on (I'm talking round about 2500 BCE – give or take a few hundred years), the women of Mesopotamia enjoyed much the same privileges as men.[13] However, there is a caveat here as when it comes to finding women in the historical record unfortunately (and this is not unique to Mesopotamia) written evidence mostly deals with the wealthy. Little is therefore known about women in the lower classes – their mentions in contemporary writings are commonly as objects of trade. We do know though that wealthy women had the money and status to act on their own. They could engage in trade or legal transactions such as borrowing or lending, and they were able to acquire property.[14] On the whole women thrived.

As this newly civilised world continued to grow, the egalitarian model of Catalhoyuk was slowly abandoned. A new one began to emerge – one that showed the beginnings of a class system and dynastic rule. The expansion of city-states brought the inevitability of war, and with this the election of physically strong men to protect them from their enemies. Rule was passed from father to son, and for the first time the rules that governed society were written down enshrining this new patriarchal system in law.

It is during the rule of Sargon the Great, just a few hundred years later, that the outlook for women drastically changed. For the first time, the silencing of women began to appear in law. Like a horrifying omen of what women's rights would become under this new system, a piece of written evidence from an attempted government reform declares that any woman brave enough to speak "out of turn" should have her teeth smashed with a brick.[15]

The new class systems brought uneven distributions of wealth and with them uneven distributions of power. In stark contrast to the freedom to act on their own, women were now passive objects living under the authority of their fathers or husbands. With their roles increasingly tied to the household, they began to be excluded from positions of power and public spaces.[16] If you're looking for the moment women became anchored to the kitchen, this is it folks. When women did work, positions such as weavers, palace administrators, or child carers kept them appropriately within the domestic space. However, their pay was just half the rations awarded to men.[17] As a quick aside, I have to say it's quite incredible to think that unequal pay stretches this far back. Even more incredible to think that it took until the 20th century to put it right – or at least attempt to. It wasn't until 1961 that Iceland, the first country in the world to address this, enshrined the right to pay equality between men and women in law. Today, other countries around the world now have similar laws – the USA brought theirs about in 1963, Australia in 1969, the UK in 1970, and Peru in 2017. These are just a handful. However, as of 2022 there are still 95 countries that do not guarantee equal pay for equal work.[18] And people wonder why women are so pissed about it. But perhaps that is for another book.

Belonging to a household group became an increasingly important part of a woman's identity. Any woman who didn't was viewed with suspicion. Women like these who'd escaped the masculine authority they were supposed to live under were considered dangerous to the social order; some even being accused of witchcraft, a crime that the peoples of Mesopotamia took very seriously.[19] This view of women outside the control of men still exists in our time. We might not call them witches these days, but women who operate outside of expected norms are still viewed with mistrust. It made me think of some of the cartoon villains I grew up watching on TV – the likes of Ursula from *The Little Mermaid*, Cruella De Vil from *101 Dalmatians*, Maleficent of *Sleeping Beauty* fame, or Madam Mim from *The Sword in the Stone*. All share similar qualities in that they are mostly loners (certainly outside of the control of a man) and on the fringes of society or its expected behaviours. They do not meet expected female beauty standards, they are confident, they are calculating. Many of them also possess power – be it magical or, in Cruella's case, influence or control over others. There is though, another quality that they are bestowed with – a quality that cautions anyone who steps outside the safe boundaries of what is expected. They are all either evil or mad. Whether they are evil or mad because they are outsiders, or they are outsiders because they are evil or mad, the same message has echoed down the millennia. Women who do not conform are dangerous.

The passage of time in Mesopotamia did not do women any favours. The historical record reflects their increasing invisibility. Fewer elite women appear in writings of the period and those that did began to be represented differently.[20] The Mesopotamian world was becoming male-dominated and contemporary art and religious representations had displays of male strength and prowess at its fore. Rulers used such propaganda to legitimise their authority. Stone carvings and reliefs showed them as powerful and strong, leading their armies, smiting their enemies, and later even triumphing over lions – the most powerful and dangerous creatures in Mesopotamia.

The divine world also reflected the change to the human world's social order. Masculine deities became raised in importance over feminine ones. The goddess figures of fertility and nature that had been so prevalent in places like Catalhoyuk became sidelined in favour of the male gods of justice and reason. The feminine pantheon now represented merely gods' wives rather than powerful beings in their own right. One goddess, the goddess Inanna, is particularly interesting. She represented carnal love, and as such had neither husband nor children. She was often portrayed as having violent outbursts of anger, a quality which also made her a formidable goddess of war.[21] This idea of women's incapacity to control their emotions and proneness to emotional and spiritual 'leakage' has stretched far beyond Mesopotamia and as we'll see has stuck with us right up to today.

Happily, the historical record wasn't solely dominated by men. One woman in particular stands out from the crowd. Enheduanna.

Enheduanna is significant because in this male-dominated world she was able to use her position to forge a route to power, and in doing so became the cultural force behind her father's throne. Daughter of Sargon the Great, Enheduanna was given an important role as the priestess to the moon god Nanna. It is worth knowing that religion played an extraordinary role in both public and private life. Its ideas influenced institutions, art, literature, and activities performed by kings and their subjects.[22] Each city had a sort of 'national god' attached to it, and each district of the city had its own god with its own temple. Rulers governed their cities on behalf of the gods and were expected to maintain and restore temples. You can imagine then the chaos that competition and disharmony between temples had the potential to cause.

As well as holding the role of priestess, Enheduanna was a poet. She is credited as the earliest known poet in history and the first author to personally identify herself through the use of the word 'I'. Having written several poems, she used her collection of hymns to the goddess Inanna to unify religious temples across the country, strengthening her father's rule.[23] Sargon is now thought to be the first person in recorded history to rule over an empire – a feat impossible without some kind of unity. Following her death Enheduanna's works continued to be used for centuries. It's likely she was remembered as an important figure, perhaps even a semi-divine one. A fleeting glimpse of feminine brilliance in an otherwise male world.

Sadly, following the likes of Enheduanna, little improved for women in Mesopotamia. In fact, it's fair to say it got markedly worse. Around 1754 BCE the Code of Hammurabi was formed. It is considered the foundation stone of world civilisation. And this is where I have a problem – from whose perspective? Certainly not women's. What the Code represents is the most comprehensive and best-preserved legal text from the ancient Near East – this was the code that gave us "an eye for an eye, a tooth for a tooth". One of its underlying principles is that people were not equal before the law (you can perhaps start to see my issue). If you skip over the beginning which outlines how Hammurabi was given rulership by the gods, then a first-person list of all his achievements and virtues (blah, blah, blah), the Code covers a broad list of laws from property offences to assault, and marriage and family, to agriculture. At some point scholars agreed this was a foundation stone of civilisation due to the perceived fairness and respect for the rule of law that it demonstrates – so much so that Hammurabi is still considered an important historical figure in law history. The US Capitol even has a relief portrait of Hammurabi alongside other historical lawgivers. It's debated as to whether the Code was actual law, a guide for formulating judgements, or whether this was propaganda portraying Hammurabi as a 'king of justice' in line with the greatest of the gods. Regardless of its actual function most scholars agree that the laws it outlines are a window into the ideology and functioning of society at the time.[24] Given that women were pretty much invisible in the historical record at this point, this window is helpful in understanding what life might have been like.

The Code paints a picture of a society where punishments varied according to the status of the victim – the main differences in status being influenced by social class and gender. The Code was a double-edged sword for women. Whilst it recognised women as individuals they were also still treated as the property of men. Their reproductive systems fell under male ownership which meant crimes like rape were an economic offence – if a woman was raped, the crime was actually against her father or husband as she was now considered devalued.[25] The Code did afford women some protections like a minimum wage and protection from ill-treatment, poverty, or neglect, but it was also very clear that the penalties for transgressions were severe and often much harsher than those given to men. Let me give you an example. Take adultery – should a man be sneaking around with another woman behind his wife's back, his punishment was to pay a fee of 20-30 shekels of silver. But, if a woman merely dared to verbally disown her husband (note, no hanky-panky with anyone else here) then she should be bound and thrown into a river. Seems disproportionate, no? In short, women could be put to death for adultery, whereas men merely had the inconvenience of a fine to pay. And the discrimination against women did not stop there.

Around 1200 BCE, with Mesopotamia under the Assyrian Empire women's freedoms were limited even further. The artwork of the period captures this total dominance of men. For those of you who have been to the British Museum in London and wandered through the Assyria gallery, you may have seen some examples of what I'm talking about. A total juxtaposition of beauty and savagery, the lion hunt reliefs of Ashurbanipal from 645-635 BCE are beautiful stone-carved reliefs that once adorned the North Palace at Ninevah. I say beautiful – and they are as the craftsmanship required to create them is awe-inspiring – but what they depict is nothing short of horrifying. I remember them vividly from my studies at university and recall seeing them for the first time outside of a textbook. My husband (then boyfriend) had taken me on a weekend to London for my birthday. We spent it doing all the touristy things I love – museums, Mr Foggs Gin Parlour, I think we even saw *The Lion King* at the theatre.

Inevitably we ended up at the British Museum. I don't think he really understood why I paused for so long in front of those reliefs. I was mesmerised. As a woman in a world where the scales are constantly tipped against you it's hard not to see yourself reflected in those lions, every day having to endure the assertion of male dominance. In the reliefs men exert not just their dominance, but violent and unmerciful control over nature. Within the scenes carved in stone, many a lioness can be seen vomiting blood or with arrows sticking out of their bodies as they collapse under the might of their hunters. As I stood there, I saw them as somehow symbolic of the women in Mesopotamia.

Gone were the few protective measures of the Code of Hammurabi. Strict regulations were introduced, and public behaviour rigidly controlled. Punishment for transgression became even more brutal – the wife of a rapist would herself be raped as punishment for her husband's action. [26] Access to women was heavily regulated, particularly within the palace walls. Outsiders were checked (likely to see if they were castrated), servants were not permitted to speak to women with bare shoulders, and if a palace woman dared to meet a man without a chaperone both would likely be killed.[27] The first veiling laws separated women by their social class. Although married women were allowed to venture outside of the home alone, they had to cover their heads. Any unmarried women, slaves, or sex workers, however, covered their heads at their peril. Doing so would see them punished with 50 lashes, have their clothes removed and hot pitch poured over their head.[28]

I think it's fair to say that women in ancient

Mesopotamia had not just been relegated to second-class citizens but had become convenient scapegoats for other people's bad behaviour. They seem to have been expected to shoulder the blame for pretty much everything. Husband mismanages her dowry and gets into debt? Her fault. Husband has an affair? Her fault. Women had gone from owning property to being property – first of their fathers, then of their husbands. If their own behaviour was less than perfect, they were punished harshly. Law had divided women into respectable and unrespectable – a theme that would permeate other cultures. The veil too would filter through the civilisations of Greece and Rome, eventually becoming a mark of social class, both limiting and protecting women in a man's world.[29]

FINDING BALANCE

In 2002 I started my first sixth-form year at college. I'd made a bit of a U-turn on my GCSE subjects and had suddenly decided that instead of studying A-level Geography, I wanted to study History. I honestly can't remember what led me to make that decision, but it's safe to say I did it not knowing just how much it would dictate the course of my life. It was a decision that led me to choose to study ancient history, a decision that landed me at the University of Birmingham, a decision that led me to make that city my home and ultimately led me to meet my close friends and my husband.

The year before I began that new chapter of my life in the second city, as Birmingham is commonly referred to (how appropriate), I was fortunate enough to travel to Egypt with my family. My parents thought it would be an incredible experience for me to have spent time in one of the places I would go onto study, and they were right. It was incredible. It was a privilege.

Over the course of several weeks, we spent time in Luxor exploring the massive temple complex of Karnak, the Valley of the Kings, Hatshepsut's temple at Deir el-Bahari and the worker's village of Deir el-Medina. Finally, we ended our trip in Cairo, taking in the Pyramids of Giza and the Egyptian Museum. It's difficult to impress on anyone yet to visit just how captivating Egypt is. With its very ancient history literally all around you, parts of it feel like a time warp – or at least it would do if it weren't for all the tourists. One evening, a few hours before sundown, I remember going down to the Nile and hiring a traditional Egyptian wooden boat with a canvas sail. Mohammad, who owned the felucca, made us sweet tea to drink and serenaded us with the occasional Beatles song as we sailed peacefully up and down. The banks of the river seemed miles away, yet we could still make out people who had come with their pots to be washed or animals to be watered. Distant shouts and laughter from children playing in the water rang out every now and then. After a while, the sun kissed the horizon and the air cooled. As if by magic, the water suddenly turned into a dazzling river of gold, the final and parting gift from the sun which had completed its daily commute across the sky. It was magical. Somewhere I have a picture of my dad sat quietly on his own at the side of the felucca, feet up and silhouetted against the golden backdrop.

Having stepped into what is left of Egypt's magnificent history for those few short weeks, it's easy to see why so many historians find it utterly fascinating. The oppression of women in male-dominated societies was by no means an inevitable outcome of civilisation. Some societies continued for centuries with relative equality between the sexes. Ancient Egypt was one of them.

The idea of balance, or maat, was central to ancient Egypt. I'm guessing at some point you've likely seen Egyptian artwork with its distinctive symmetry (yes, *The Mummy* movie franchise totally counts).[30] Well, this idea of balance was evident in gender roles within Egypt too – so much so that Herodotus, the ancient Greek historian, believed that the Egyptians had reversed the ordinary practices of mankind (which kind of gives the game away about the ancient Greeks' attitude towards women, but more on that later).[31]

Like Mesopotamia, ancient Egypt had a social hierarchy. However, the crucial difference here was that your rights depended more on your class than they did on your gender.

Evidence from artwork, grave goods, and contemporary writings all point to a society where women had reasonable autonomy. A tomb at Saqqara shows a woman steering a cargo ship whilst ordering a man to get her food.[32] Women are also shown trading at markets; they could buy and sell property and bring actions to court. Surviving contracts and accounts even show that women received the same pay rations as men for doing the same job. Yep, the ancient Egyptians had achieved something we're still waiting for in too many countries today.

Contemporary reliefs and paintings show husbands and wives together, eating, drinking, and working the fields. It's a fair argument to say that Egyptian art is highly idealised, but like the artwork of Mesopotamia, it does seem to broadly reflect the society it comes from. And in Egypt women had a greater social standing than in many other ancient (and indeed modern) societies.[33]

However, despite what seems like a reasonably fair deal (at least in comparison with Mesopotamia) we have to acknowledge that women in Egypt were still serving a patriarchy. The Divine Kingship of the pharaohs passed through sons, not daughters, and men occupied the vast majority of positions of power and authority.

Ironically, it is because of the importance placed on the Divine Kingship that Egypt gives us some of the most extraordinary women rulers who, despite the system, rose to power and reigned successfully. The survival of Egypt was paramount to the ancient Egyptians and deeply tied to that was the Divine Kingship and the sense of strength and endurance it created. Therefore, on occasion it was accepted that female rulers were sometimes the necessary placeholders of men. A female pharaoh was far better than no pharaoh at all. Egyptians understood that women ruled differently and in times of potential peril, for example where a male heir was too young to rule, women offered a stability that men often didn't. In essence, women weren't taking unnecessary risks or rushing to war.[34] Instead, they offered more nurturing, compassionate leadership qualities in times of great need.

Now, before you call me out on stereotyping here, bear with me as it turns out that the Egyptians may have been onto something. Whilst undertaking research into their book *The Athena Doctrine* published in 2013, John Gerzema and Michael D'Antonio found that of the 64,000 people they surveyed across

13 different countries, two thirds of them thought the world would be a better place if men thought more like women. Essentially, what these guys turned up was a global referendum on men. You may think I'm joking, I'm not. Gerzema and D'Antonio were intrigued by the growing shift between masculine and feminine values in areas like what people want from their leaders. As well as their extensive survey, they interviewed CEOs, start-ups, entrepreneurs, and the boardrooms of Fortune 500 companies. They observed that the most innovative people amongst us were breaking away from traditional masculine 'winner takes all' approaches towards being more flexible, nurturing, and collaborative – what they call the Athena Doctrine. As part of their research, they looked at how the world categorises various traits as either masculine, feminine, or neutral, and which traits are associated with things like leadership, happiness, and morality. The results were clear. People believed that femininity would make the world a better place. Traits commonly associated with women – traits like empathy, collaboration, intuition, patience, and future-focus – were recognised as of significant value in bringing success to people and organisations across the world.[35] Classic codes of male conduct like control, aggression, black-and-white thinking, and risk-taking were no longer seen as *the* route to success.

Perhaps this is what the Egyptians had recognised several thousand years before us. Despite the obvious misalignment with their patriarchal structure, they understood the value in female leadership – at least enough to tolerate it when the going got tough. In these tough times Egypt gave us examples of women who not only managed to achieve the power and authority of high office but carry their country through adversity.

The first of these many examples I'd like to introduce is Queen Sobeknefru. Around 1805 BCE, Sobeknefru inherited the throne following her husband's death. Whilst she may have reigned for only a few short years, her brilliance was in using the masculine trappings of royalty to legitimise her own reign. If you're getting 1980s 'power dressing' vibes you'd be absolutely bang on. It seems women have been having to dress and behave like to men to legitimise their own power for a long time. In a similar way to women of the '80s wearing big shoulder pads designed to emulate the larger, squarer male figure, a damaged statue of Sobeknefru shows her in a combination of both men's and women's dress. Not satisfied in leaving her physical image to do the talking, Sobeknefru also used masculine titles to cement her authority as ruler instead of those reserved for queens. For its time, this attempt to silence any critics of women's leadership using masculine symbols of power was pretty bold.[36] All of this must have worked, as the very fact that her name is included on Egyptian king lists suggests her reign was accepted by the people and historians that preserved her memory.[37]

The next woman I want to introduce is a bit of a hero of mine – Hatshepsut. Daughter of Thutmose I, Hatshepsut was of royal bloodline but as a female of the royal family would never have been expected to rule. Yet, The King Herself (as she preferred to be called) reigned between 1479 – 1458 BCE. She had initially come to the throne as queen regent, ruling until her stepson Thutmose III came of age. Acting on his behalf she respectfully complied with convention and handled the political affairs of the country. However, within a few years Hatshepsut was reigning as 'King of Egypt' – something she continued to do for over two decades.[38] This was highly unusual, and we may never know what made Hatshepsut decide to break with tradition, but one thing is for sure – she knew how to do it well.

Once she had made that decision to transform herself into a King, there was only one model she could follow – that of Sobeknefru. Hatshepsut legitimised her reign, not through links to her deceased pharaoh husband, but through her own divine bloodline. And like Enheduanna, she used the ideology of the time to her advantage. By taking the title 'God's Wife' instead of 'King's Wife' she elevated her status to that of the divine. Knowing that Divine Kingship passed from father to son, this link to divinity despite her sex would have been powerful in paving her way to the throne.[39] Similarly to Sobeknefru, Hatshepsut never hid her sex, but instead shrewdly used it. She harnessed the male symbols of power – the pharaonic headdress and false beard – in her imagery in an attempt to synthesize king and queen and create unassailable power for herself.

Hatshepsut had been born into a dynasty that saw Egypt still reeling from a hundred years of Hyksos rule, foreign kings on the throne, and civil unrest. However, her reign was characterised not by war but by exploration, leaving Egypt in a better state than she had found it. Hatshepsut's exploratory campaigns enlarged Egypt's empire beyond anything it had previously seen with trade missions bringing back luxury goods, gold, and incense.[40] Her reign brought economic prosperity to Egypt. She embarked on great building projects, raising temples and renovating shrines. She left hundreds of statues of herself, magnificent obelisks, and accounts in stone of her lineage and history – both real and imagined (the ancient equivalent of Instagram versus reality). [41] But 20 years after her death, Thutmose III, who was now Pharaoh, set about obliterating her memory and chiselling away her name and image as King. Why? Perhaps to legitimise his own right to rule? Revenge for 20 years of wounded male pride and a throne robbed? We may never know. However, we shouldn't underestimate just how serious this campaign to eradicate Hatshepsut's memory was. Removing all traces of Hatshepsut allowed the literal re-writing of history. *History isn't what happened. It's who tells the story.* The succession of the throne now ran from Thutmose I to Thutmose III without female interference. This campaign also served another purpose – the destruction of her spirit or the 'second death'. With no image, name, or memory left on Earth, the spirit of the deceased Hatshepsut would also perish and be lost forever. Unlike Sobeknefru who had ruled at the end of a fading dynasty, Hatshepsut's reign had brought prosperity to Egypt. It may simply be that a successful woman on the throne isn't something the Egyptians wanted repeated as this threatened the delicate balance so central to their thinking and culture.[42]

The conundrum of Hatshepsut, who she was, and what her motives were, have continued through the centuries. Her reign and her character have undergone radical transformations in the eyes of historians – from a good ruler simply holding the fort, to a throne-stealing 'wicked stepmother' figure. This black-and-white thinking about women in power is something that crops up again and again. Modern assessments of her seem more balanced, accepting that she was neither wholly good nor wholly bad. She was in fact, human. Whilst it's impossible for any writer to totally divorce themselves from their subjects, Hatshepsut does seem to provoke a particularly personal response in many, such is the power of her legacy.

Hatshepsut wasn't the end of powerful women in Egypt. Following her, several women achieved powerful roles – Queen Tiy who was politically active during her husband's reign, Nefertiti the well-known beauty who was often depicted alongside her husband and is thought by some to have been almost as powerful as Pharaoh himself. And Ankhesenamun, wife of Tutankhamun, who upon being widowed was independent enough to arrange a new marriage in an attempt to secure her position and her safety.[43]

For a civilisation that did not relish women in power, it produced some impressive female rulers. And on that note, it wouldn't be right to finish a chapter on ancient Egypt without mention of possibly the most famous female pharaoh of them all – Cleopatra VII. You would be forgiven for thinking that all Cleopatra had to offer was a beautiful face and a temptresses body – after all, Hollywood has turned her story into movie gold and her name is now synonymous with that of Elizabeth Taylor. As is true for all women, Cleopatra was far more than just her looks. Was she a beauty? Debatable. Was she witty and charming? Probably. Was she a shrewd politician who used her intelligence and gender to further her own interests? Certainly. Her ability to charm some of the most powerful men the world has ever known would lead her to the throne, but sadly also to her death.

Cleopatra's reign came at a time of instability. Born in 69 BCE, she was a member of an ancient Greek dynasty that had been ruling Egypt since it was conquered by Alexander the Great. Like Hatshepsut, she came to the throne after her father's death, ruling alongside her brother Ptolemy XIII. Unfortunately for Cleopatra, her path to power was not as smooth. Her brother was set on having the throne for himself and civil war soon broke out between the siblings, forcing Cleopatra into exile. In an effort to retake Egypt for herself, she turned to another powerhouse for support – Rome, and Julius Caesar.

Developing strategic relationships with powerful men was something that Cleopatra excelled at. She chose those that could bring something to her table. To Caesar, Cleopatra would have been highly unusual, and likely quite overwhelming in comparison to Roman women. Cleopatra was empowered, confident, and intelligent, and Caesar would have been able to talk with her about military campaigns, politics, literature, and philosophy on almost equal terms. Knowing that a positive alliance with Rome would ensure Egypt's survival, Cleopatra began a relationship with Caesar. It was a relationship that not only won her back her throne, but one in which she developed considerable influence over him and Roman politics. In fact, we still feel her influence today in the form of our calendar. It was her guidance that helped Caesar adjust what was at the time an ineffective Roman calendar to one with twelve months of the year, each with 30 days.

Cleopatra's affair with Caesar didn't just bring her

influence and security, it also produced a son, Caesarion. This would not be the last time Cleopatra strategically used her sex and reproductive capabilities to cement power and create a legacy for herself. Following Caesar's assassination in 44 BCE, Cleopatra set her sights on another Roman political player – Mark Antony. In an effort to maintain the Egyptian–Roman alliance, she set out to impress by arriving at a meeting in Tarsus (modern-day Turkey) on a sumptuous barge, wearing expensive gowns, jewels, and burning exotic incense. It worked.

Antony and Cleopatra soon began a love affair that saw Antony leave Rome and move to Egypt to be with her. But Cleopatra wasn't just set on winning the hearts and minds of powerful men – she wanted the love of the Egyptian people too. Her ability to speak multiple languages, including Egyptian, as well as her interest in practising Egyptian religion would have transformed her from a Greek on the Egyptian throne into an Egyptian queen. And for just over a decade, she remained exactly that – Queen of Egypt. Her reign turned Egypt's fortunes around. She increased exports and employment, the economy boomed, her people loved her.

However, Cleopatra had made the wrong decision in a Roman power struggle. After suffering a massive defeat at the hands of his enemy Octavian (who would go on to become the first Emperor of Rome), Antony fell on his sword and eventually died in Cleopatra's arms. After burying Mark Antony in her own tomb, she knew it was likely that Octavian would take her back to Rome as a prisoner and parade her through the streets in triumph. To avoid this humiliation and almost certain death in a foreign land, Cleopatra chose to take her own life.

Sadly, the relative equality enjoyed by women in Egypt came to an end around a hundred years after Cleopatra's death. Her canny decision-making had brought a brief period of peace and economic stability to an otherwise chaotic Egypt.[44] Her undoing was her unwavering support of the wrong man.

The Proper Way

Gender roles, stereotypes, and assumptions are littered throughout our everyday lives. Just Google image search 'builder' and you'll have to scroll down a way past all the men before you see a picture of a human woman (yes, believe it or not we are nestled amongst cartoons of ourselves). Whereas, if you search 'secretary' the opposite is true.

A recent run-in of my own with gender stereotyping happened not long after the purchase of my first house with my husband. At the time I was a 37-year-old mother of one in the middle of my maternity leave. We'd moved into a new-build estate and because of this received regular visits from all sorts of people trying to sell us anything from takeaways to window cleaning, landscaping to solar panels. One day I was at home alone trying to get some jobs done whilst my son napped and decided to call my sister for a catch up. Part way through our conversation the doorbell rang. On answering the door with one hand, phone in the other, I was greeted by a smiley middle-aged man, smartly dressed and carrying a bunch of leaflets. "Hello" he said politely. "Is your mum or dad in?" I couldn't honestly tell you how long this man waited for me to respond. I think I was stunned into silence. The thing I remember most about this interaction, funnily enough, wasn't the ludicrous question I'd just been asked, it was hearing my sister's hysterical tinny laughter coming out of the phone in my hand. "Are you kidding me?" I asked, not really looking for him to answer, "I own the place!" I have never seen a person look more embarrassed. He stuttered and stumbled for a way out, but we both knew it was a fruitless task and after several profuse apologies, I shut the door. I didn't buy his services.

Faced with a short woman wearing jogging bottoms and a t-shirt when the door to my house opened, that man's assumption was 'this is not the homeowner or decision maker'. I doubt it was even a conscious one, so ingrained are these gender stereotypes. As we've seen so far, ancient society's expectations of women and the role they played – or were supposed to play – has been revealed through contemporary artwork, laws, and monuments. Ancient China's relationship with gender is particularly apparent in its philosophy and literature. Ideas about specific gender roles within a patriarchal system are no more overt than those of the philosopher Confucius. Although his ideas didn't take root in his lifetime, following his death they became China's dominant philosophy and continue to have a huge impact today.

So, who was Confucius? If you've heard sayings like "Our

greatest glory is not in never falling, but in rising every time we fall" and "It does not matter how slowly you go, as long as you do not stop", well, that's him. Given that his ideas had such an influence on Chinese thinking around gender roles, it's probably fair to spend a bit of time introducing the guy. Confucius was born in the year 551 BCE into a class somewhere between the aristocracy and the common people. Not only was this a formative period in China's intellectual history, but it was also a time of war between feudal states. This context likely inspired Confucius to create his doctrine outlining a way of life that he believed would restore peace and social order. He considered himself to be a transmitter of values from an earlier time that had long been forgotten. Confucian philosophy put an emphasis on morality, the correctness of social relationships, justice, and virtue. It placed the family at the cornerstone of society with a deeply hierarchical structure – the top relationships being father to son, and women at the bottom of the pile.[45] His ideas provided guidance and rules of conduct for people and the government in fulfilling their responsibilities towards others. And although Confucius says very little about women, what he does say is revealing:

"It is not pleasing to have to do with women or people of base condition" [46]

Lovely.

By neglecting to define the role of women, or even say much about them at all, Confucius left the door open for others to make their own interpretations. One interpretation is that this general lack of reference to women means that they were to be ignored. However, given that women make up half the population this would have been pretty unrealistic. Instead, rather than simply ignoring them, some form of control would become necessary to preserve the proper way of life.

This idea of a 'proper way' shaped the experiences of women in ancient China and for centuries onwards. It became intertwined with an ancient concept of balance outlined in the *I Ching*, a Chinese divination text. Balance in society was believed to be reflected in the balance of the cosmos. Therefore, any imbalance in the human world was thought to cause the heavens to wreak havoc with plagues, famine, and political collapse.[47] Not ideal. Linked to this was the concept of Yin and Yang – opposite but complementary and connected forces. On one side you have Yin, standing for the female and all things dark and hidden. On the other, Yang, standing for the male and all things bright, warm, and overt.[48] The Yin Yang symbol – a circle divided in two, one half black, the other white; both halves containing a smaller circle of the other – represents this balance between two opposites. Neither side is superior to the other, but both exist in a dynamic system. To support the proper way, this concept would need to be reimagined and remoulded.

Born hundreds of years after Confucius, Dong Zhongshu was the scholar and philosopher that merged the Confucian and Yin Yang schools of thought. It was his work that established Confucianism as the state philosophy of China – a position it held for two thousand years.[49] As a result of his reinterpretation of Yin Yang, the balance central to this concept disappeared. Yin became seen as inferior to Yang. The impact of this on women was massive. Now, the inferiority of the female was part of the natural order of things and the subordination of women validated.[50] Suddenly patriarchy wasn't manmade, but divinely ordained. The age-old story of men giving themselves the benefit of having God on their side.[51]

Later interpretations of Confucianism reinforced male authority and the subservience of women as the proper, natural order which women expressed through their roles as wives and mothers. To maintain balance with men's place in public life, a woman's proper place became hidden away in the home. Under these later interpretations women had three roles: sexual object and possession of men, child-bearing tool, and servant to the whole family.[52] Through these roles, women could attain some semblance of honour and power. A wife's loyalty to her husband was deeply praised. The highest achievable status was to become a mother – especially to sons who would carry on her husband's family name. Daughters were seen as an economic burden due to their only use being to the family household they would eventually marry into. A daughter's blood family wouldn't see any benefit of time and money spent on her education or personal growth. Confucian philosophy even suggested that the virtue of a woman was her lack of knowledge and talent – so why invest in it?[53]

This hidden role of women wasn't just physical in that she remained tucked away in the family home. Once married, that hiddenness extended to her identity. She became nameless, her given and maiden names forgotten. Instead, she would be known as 'daughter-in-law of the Wang family' or 'big mother of the Wang family'.[54]

Confucian ideas didn't stop at influencing male thinkers, historians, and scholars. Ban Zhao, one of the first known female Chinese historians, accepted the idea that men were superior and built on this to create her highly popular and influential work *Lessons for Women*. This addressed the void left by Confucius's silence on women by serving for centuries as a practical set of guidelines for women's everyday conduct. Ban Zhao suggested that women had no need to be intelligent, clever of speech, attractive, or even particularly talented, but instead should practice respect for The Three Obediences: to father, then husband, then upon husband's death to eldest son; and The Four Virtues: morality, proper speech, modest manner, diligent work. Adherence to these would provide women with a proper way to behave and, crucially, maintain the social order.[55]

Another popular literary work written by two female scholars expanded on Ban Zhao's views. The *Analects for Women* enshrined the notion of separate spheres for men and women – men existed in the outer sphere of business and politics, and women in the inner sphere of the home and childcare. It warned against learning from women whose behaviours and attitudes contradicted the proper way. Those who ignored this advice risked bringing shame and disgrace upon themselves and their family.[56]

Over centuries a whole body of literature was written and compiled to educate women on self-discipline, etiquette, and relationships. Whilst I don't believe the primary intent of Confucian philosophy was the oppression of women, it's undeniable that its principles have contributed to it. These ideas of loyalty and obedience to husband and in-laws above all else prevailed right up until the 20th century and became a defining hallmark of Chinese civilisation.[57]

So deeply embedded did Confucian philosophy become in China, and more widely across East Asia, that its effects can still be felt today. Despite increasing numbers of Chinese women in education and more intense interest in feminist issues, young women are feeling the pressure from parents and relatives who hold traditional ideals to make personal, financial, and career sacrifices in favour of marriage and childbearing. Yet more and more young women are shunning tradition, reluctant to give up their personal freedoms. Women's choices not to marry or have children have seen the last decade's marriage and birth rates plummet – in fact, in 2022 China's population shrank for the first time in sixty years.[58] This is a problem for China as it now faces a male-dominated, aging population which will have a significant impact on its future economic, social, and demographic stability. Historic policies designed to control a rapidly increasing population limited the number of children couples could have. Recent reversals of those policies have not yielded the baby boom the ruling Chinese Communist Party hoped for. Women are exercising more freedom and control over their lives, which flies in the face of the Party's plans for a new type of marriage and childbearing culture – one that they're desperately trying to encourage through cash handouts and tax benefits. [59]

Subjugating women and a return to old values around women's roles once again looks to be the vehicle through which China is hoping to modernise and deal with the population problem. The potential implications for women's rights, as you can imagine, are enormous.

Despite Confucian doctrine defining women's roles and behaviours as domestic, unseen, and obedient, the arrival of Buddhism around 200 BCE – 200 CE and its ideas about the irrelevancy of gender offered women an alternative way.[60] One person who turned this to her advantage was the Empress Wu Zetian.

Empress Wu Zetian leveraged this other way to found her own dynasty in the 7th century CE, ruling for 15 years in her own right – the only woman in 3000 years of Chinese history to do so. Empress Wu succeeded in stabilising the crumbling Tang dynasty, considered the golden age of Chinese civilisation. Little is known about her early life, but what we do know is that she managed to elevate herself from a low rank and enter into the palace as a consort, and from there into the emperor's affections. Establishing herself as her husband's equal, she became a heavy influence behind the throne and, following his death, an influence behind the reign of her sons. Eventually, in 690 CE she ordered the last of her sons to abdicate and took power for herself.[61]

Unlike the Egyptian women who used male dress and accessories to validate their positions in power, Wu used the idea of personally embodying the balance of the cosmos to justify hers. To achieve this, she created a unique alphabetic character by taking the symbols for the sun (representing the male) and the moon (representing the female) and combining them with the symbol of the earth. By integrating this new character into her name, Wu implied that she was more than a female, embodying a balance of Yin and Yang in an existence beyond her sex.[62]

How successful or moral in character Empress Wu Zetian was has been debated by historians. It is perhaps because of this ambiguity that I find her a particularly fascinating example of a brilliant woman from ancient history. There are several reasons for such debate about her reign, the main one being heavily biased surviving sources for us to go on. Imperial history was written to provide lessons for future rulers, and so tended to be prejudiced against usurpers or anyone who upset Confucian sensibilities.[63] Other sources were written by her relatives who, perhaps not surprisingly, weren't exactly die-hard fans. Wu herself was also not averse to tampering with the historical record.

Her reign therefore is often viewed as one of two extremes. For centuries it has been painted as one of terror. Tales of poisoning, deviancy, and outright murder of those who threatened her power – including family members – are widely acknowledged. However, there's also a view that her reign was a peaceful one, that she cut taxes, gave retirees a pension, expanded the Chinese empire, raised the salaries of deserving officials, and turned royal land over to husbandry. *History isn't what happened. It's who tells the story.*

While historians debate who Wu really was, Confucian philosophy says that while an emperor shouldn't be condemned for acts that might be considered a crime in a commoner, they should be judged harshly for letting the state fall into anarchy.[64] In that respect, it's fair to consider her rule a success. Perhaps the reason she was so reviled for so long is down to the double standards used to assess male and female rulers. Wu was a ruler of her time. Few Chinese emperors came to power and stayed there without the use of violence and a ruthless approach to rivals and critics. Had Empress Wu Zetian been *Emperor* Wu Zetian, I suspect that her actions would have been unlikely to attract the same criticism.

Upon Wu's death and the collapse of the Tang Dynasty, historians blamed women for invoking the wrath of the heavens. Chinese history has invariably set aside women like Empress Wu. Her kind served as a warning – anyone who went against the proper way risked disturbing the balance of the cosmos and should not be tolerated; certainly not celebrated. Perhaps for this reason, her giant stone memorial on the road to her tomb remains blank. Here are echoes of Hatshepsut and Egyptian attempts to obliterate the name of their most successful female ruler. Wu's is the only known uncarved memorial stone in 2000 years of Chinese imperial history – which tells you something about how following generations viewed her after her death. We will probably never know the truth about Empress Wu Zetian, but the fact that she existed and achieved what she did despite the odds stacked against her is enough for me.

Lessons Learned

In 2020 during the COVID-19 pandemic, like many people I was stuck at home under lockdown and watching a *lot* of TV. During that period, a documentary landed on Netflix called *Athlete A*. It chronicled the story of American athletes who had suffered sexual abuse at the hands of Larry Nassar, one of the team doctors used by USA Gymnastics for the women's gymnastics team. As the documentary unfolded, it became clear that the women bravely facing the cameras to tell their story were not alone. Larry Nassar had perpetrated a pattern of abuse against more than one hundred young women and girls over the course of almost thirty years.

How on earth did this happen, you might ask? Because the adults responsible for hiring Nassar, the adults responsible for the safety and wellbeing of those young women and girls, failed to listen when they spoke out. They believed him over them. And so Nassar remained, his decades of sexual abuse only coming to an end because several of his victims felt able to speak out on their own. During his sentencing in 2018, Judge Rosemarie Aquilina did something extraordinary. She made everybody listen – including Larry Nassar. She invited all those women abused by him to deliver victim impact statements if they chose. And they did – some alone, some in groups, some addressed Nassar directly, some via their families. Judge Aquilina supported each one with kind words, telling one Olympic gold medallist, "I'm an adult. I'm listening. I'm sorry it took this long".

Over the last few years discussions within the medical profession around women's health complaints being routinely dismissed have resurfaced. Medical professionals have begun to acknowledge that women are not being listened to or believed, their symptoms more likely to be written off as anxiety or being 'all in their head.'

You may be thinking, what has this got to do with ancient Greece, our next foray into history? Ancient Greece is considered one of history's great civilised societies – so much so that its influence is still felt globally today. We use and have built upon ancient Greek ideas in philosophy, science, and maths. Greek art and mythology heavily influenced ancient Rome and modern art theories. The ancient Greeks gave us the basis of the English alphabet, democracy, and the modern Olympics. They also gave us the original silenced woman – Cassandra.

Cassandra is also, I would argue, the original example of gaslighting – where a person is psychologically manipulated into questioning their own sanity. Hear me out. Cassandra was a mythical princess of the city of Troy and the most beautiful daughter of King Priam and Queen Hecuba. Because of this, she was admired by both mortals and immortals – in particular, the god Apollo, who tried to win her love by promising her the gift of prophecy. After bestowing this divine power upon her, Apollo then attempted to seduce Cassandra. When she refused his advances, he became enraged and spat a curse into her mouth. This curse meant that Cassandra would retain her gifted foresight, but now no-one would listen to her or believe her prophesies. And so, when she foresaw the fall of Troy and the death of her brothers, she warned her fellow Trojans against accepting the enormous wooden horse waiting outside the city gates, knowing that destruction would follow. Her warnings went ignored, Troy fell, and she was eventually driven mad by her curse.

For all those women who have ever been gaslit, accused of being melodramatic, or had their experiences dismissed, Cassandra represents a reality lived on a daily basis by women around the world. But whilst Cassandra might be one of the most famous figures of ancient Greek mythology, is she a fair representation of the lived experience of real ancient Greek women?

The definition of a civilised society according to the *Cambridge Dictionary* is one that "has a well-developed system of government, culture, and way of life and that treats the people who live there fairly."[65] We can almost certainly say that ancient Greece ticks off the first three, but what about treating people fairly? You may expect (and why wouldn't you?) that the birthplace of western democracy would also tick this final box. I certainly did. After all, the word democracy is often synonymous with fairness. However, given what I've just told you about Cassandra, you have probably twigged that the treatment of women and their representation within ancient Greek society was not as you might have expected. I'm probably being quite generous in saying it was poor at best. To understand the *why* behind women's place in Greek society, we have to appreciate some of the core ideas that underpinned Greek identity. Here begineth a quick history lesson.

Around the 6th century BCE, the dominant powers in the Near East were the Persian Empire and the Greek city states. Over decades there were a series of conflicts between these two superpowers. The Persian Empire, which began from a collection of semi-nomadic tribes, incorporated ideas from this way of life into their empire. The Greek city states, and Athens in particular, therefore defined themselves in complete opposition to their barbarian foes. If the Persians were viewed as uncivilised nomads, then the Athenians saw themselves as socially organised city-dwellers.

In 447 BCE, to celebrate the coming together of the Greek city states to vanquish their Persian invaders, Athens began an ambitious building campaign on the Acropolis above the city. The now world-famous Parthenon with its hand-carved reliefs displaying Greek victories against their enemies became an impressive architectural statement about who the Athenians were. What is depicted in the Parthenon's reliefs is deeply revealing of Athenian attitudes and how they saw social order and civilised society. Take the west side of the building as an example. It showed the Greeks fighting the Amazons – a mythical race of female warriors immortalised in Homer's *Iliad* – which, recent evidence suggests, were based on real nomadic tribes living on the Eurasian Steppe. Independent and free, the Amazonian women were the antithesis of civilisation and are shown subjugated and slaughtered by the mighty Greek male – the victory of civilisation over a barbarian monstrosity.[66]

As well as their beliefs about what constituted a civilised society, the ancient Greeks held core beliefs about the dynamic between men and women. Similarly to Confucianist ideas, they believed that women's inferiority was not man-made but rooted elsewhere. Rather than being rooted in the cosmos though, the ancient Greeks believed that female inferiority lay in their biology. Hesiod's *Works & Days*, written around two centuries before the Parthenon was built, introduces Pandora – the first woman on earth sent as a punishment to men. Described by Hesiod as the first of her species, Pandora – the "irresistible feminine weapon" that she was – arrived in the mortal realm with her box containing all the evils of the world.[67] Now, you may have heard what follows – Pandora, out of curiosity, opens said box and ends earthly paradise by releasing disease, violence, old age, greed, and other vices that would plague humankind forevermore. Awkward. What you may not know is that the word in the poem which we understand to be 'box' is 'pithos', which is the Greek word for jar. This mistranslation matters as it exposes how this perceived weakness in women was seen as biological. The ancient Greeks believed a women's womb to be shaped like a pithos. What that leaves us with is Pandora arriving with her womb, which when opened (presumably through sexual intercourse) spills out all the evils of the world.[68] As a poem intended to deliver moral instruction to its audience, these ideas about women's unbounded sexual appetites and dangerous leakage of evil through sex and menstruation penetrated the Greek psyche and became central to the Greeks' understanding of themselves, and women in particular.

Poetry, plays, and literature performed something of a parallel role in the Greek world, presenting audiences with reflections of society, ideals, and centuries of stereotyped images of women. Through literature and legend, the ancient Greeks learned that women fell into one of two categories: 'honest' or 'other'. Honest women lived in obedience within a household governed by men. The others lived alone. Women's behaviour was understood according to these categories. For instance, if an honest woman was caught in a compromising situation – say, that a husband has found her in the arms of her lover – it might be assumed that she had been seduced by some irresistible force. But if other women behaved the same way, they would be labelled as seductresses.[69] Take Helen of Troy from Homer's *Iliad* and Medea who features in myths like 'Jason and the Argonauts' and Euripides's tragedy *Medea*. Helen, the most beautiful woman in the world, was lured away from her husband by the goddess Aphrodite as a bribe for Paris, the Prince of Troy. As a high-status woman with a divine bloodline, Helen falls into the 'honest' category. Whether you interpret Helen's journey to Troy with Paris as an elopement or abduction, her adulterous behaviour is explained away though forces beyond her control.

In contrast, we have Medea. Having fallen in love with Jason, Medea uses her abilities as a sorceress to help him on his quest to regain the throne from his uncle by stealing a magical golden fleece. In the process, she abandons her home in Colchis and the pair flee to Corinth. When Jason then runs off to marry a Corinthian princess, Medea's love turns to rage, and she plots to exact her murderous revenge. Like Helen, Medea is of divine lineage and the daughter of a King. But there is one crucial difference. Medea is a foreigner, a marginalised group in ancient Greece (alongside women of course). Medea is the 'other'. Her first great speech in Euripides's play even outlines the plight of women in Greece and describes them as the worst treated things alive.[70] Medea is given no such excuse as divine intervention for her behaviour, but instead it is explained away through her otherness – her outspoken character and inability to control her emotions. Medea is the epitome of un-Greek-like behaviour. Jason even calls her a barbarian woman because of it.

So how did these ideas about women translate to ordinary life? Were women's 'biological incapabilities' merely the stuff of stories, or did these perceptions run deeper? A closer examination of ancient Greek law suggests that Athenian women were not only second-class but tightly controlled. Their reality was one of citizen status, but without the function. Athenian democracy was open to men only. Women had no place in politics, no voice, and little economic independence. Although not physically secluded, they were essentially barred from public life. Outside of the home women were often accompanied by the men of their household. The place of the civilised, honest woman was firmly at home, living peacefully (silently) under life-long male guardianship and authority. This ideal is an obvious and deliberate contrast to the barbarian, independent Amazons. Ancient Greek women were valued for their obedience, chastity, and their primary function – their ability to bear sons to continue the family line.[71] Given women's perceived inability to regulate their emotions or think with reason, men were required to do it for them. This male control left them with little choice or decision-making abilities when it came to personal affairs like marriage or money. Men had the right to decide who a woman married, which inevitably led to their treatment as passive objects married off to secure status or ties with the right families. Status and ideas of honour and shame were incredibly important to the ancient Athenians. Women embodied the honour of their household. Their behaviour was a reflection of it, and therefore any transgression they made – whether that be speaking out or exposing their bodies – was subsequently projected directly onto their husbands or fathers. Previously the right of royal women and a marker of class, by 5th century BCE the wife of nearly every citizen wore a veil as a visual symbol of her married status. The veil became a marker of ownership, but it had another more symbolic, and perhaps less well-known function too – it represented a binding of these problematic, miasmic, pithos-bearing women who leaked impurities, sexual appetites, and emotional urges.

Eventually laws codified the stereotypes of honest versus other in a way that had real consequences for ancient Greek women. In a world that valued men first, punishments for a crime committed against a woman considered not just her status, but the status of her male relatives.[72] For example, rape was considered an offence against the men who had guardianship over her. This of course applied only to honest women – the others could be assaulted with impunity.

Several hundred years after Hesiod and Homer, the philosopher Aristotle developed these long-held ideas about women, their role, and their capabilities further. In his work *Politics,* he justified women's status as second-class citizens. Although he conceded that women possessed the ability to deliberate and to reason, he suggested this ability was untrustworthy, invalid, and indecisive. Because of this, men were required to validate their decisions, actions, and take control over their matters. Aristotle believed women were sub-male – essentially, imperfect men. Males, he thought, were the real creators of life, using their reproductive cells to turn female matter into human beings. Women, on the other hand, suffered from their reproductive system – specifically their uterus – wandering around their body causing an excess of emotion. This, he suggested, was the principal reason that men were by nature "fitter for command than the female".[73] His deeply incorrect theories about the female body and its reproductive role set the tone for centuries of inferior treatment. Even Charles Darwin, best known for his contributions to evolutionary biology, would later publicly state that evolution had made men superior to women.

Today these misconceptions continue to be weaponised against women. I'm fairly confident every one of you reading this will have, at some point in your life, heard a woman ridiculed for being 'hysterical' (and by suggestion, unnecessary and extreme). Rarely is this kind of label warranted, but more usually it is an attempt to write off and discredit women's emotional responses. Well, guess what – 'hysteria' comes from the ancient Greek 'hystera', meaning uterus. It wasn't until 1980 that hysteria as a medical diagnosis, which included symptoms such as hallucinations, emotional outbursts, and delirium amongst others, was removed from the *Diagnostic and Statistical Manual of Mental Disorders* (DSM). Thanks, Aristotle.

So, what might we learn from ancient Greece about how women's place in society has been shaped? Firstly, stories are powerful and enduring. Secondly, so are beliefs about women's bodies. Both these things – stories and biology – had a profound impact on women's lived experiences in ancient Greece. Stories demonstrated the difference between the civilised and the uncivilised, the honest and the other, and strongly hinted at which side of that line women should strive to be. An independent and empowered woman was an uncivilised and dangerous one. Understanding of women's biology, however incorrect, was pivotal in creating myths around female inferiority and capability which kept women out of positions of power and under the control of men. Women in ancient Greece were trophies to be owned and found themselves voiceless, dependent, and conforming.

Some of these ancient beliefs about women have trickled down into the 21st century and continue to impact our own lives – like the idea that women are prone to emotional overstimulation. We're no more emotional than men – fact. Yet this idea persists. Looking at women in ancient Greece you could be forgiven for feeling downbeat or believing that there is little hope in changing so many centuries of women's narrative. However, like the last thing left in Pandora's box after all the evils of the world spilled out, we can find – nestled amongst the ancient stories and beliefs – some hope.

There *is* hope to be found in these ancient stories if we stop looking at them through the male lens. The hope I glimpse in the stories of Cassandra and Medea and Helen is in the consequences of underestimating them and their power. Cassandra – disbelieved and disregarded, she epitomises the plight of women in ancient Greece. Viewing her in a new light, Cassandra evolves from the silenced woman into a warning to society. Ignore women at your peril. She had a voice, but nobody listened. She had intelligence but no agency. The consequence of ignoring Cassandra was the destruction of Troy. Helen, whom the whole story of *The Iliad* – one of the great ancient literary works – hinges upon, is the very reason men go to war, fight, and die in the epic poem. She isn't a trophy, but the catalyst for change. Even Medea, tragic figure though she is, is pivotal to Jason's success in stealing the golden fleece. Without her independence and intelligence, Jason would have died trying. These mythical women were 3D – fully rounded individuals with flaws and failings. Intelligent but manipulative, powerful but violent, full of both love and cruelty. Despite the odds stacked against them, they continued their fight – Cassandra did not give up voicing her visions, just as Medea did not give up when Jason betrayed her. And neither do their stories. They have transcended generations, cultures, and continents. They endure.

These tales offer hope that women's stories – our stories – are not yet done. That there is potential there waiting to be unleashed. That the social inequalities and expectations that shape women's experiences will not hold us back from being heard, or from achieving power and agency in a world designed for men.

Doing it differently

In stark contrast to the male-dominated ancient Greece were the tribes of the Eurasian Steppes. Probably less well known than the ancient cultures of Egypt, Greece, or Rome, but no less important, these tribes represented a different way of life. Over millennia this vast area of grassland stretching from Hungary to China was a key route of travel and trade, and home to nomadic tribes like the Scythians, Mongols, and Huns. Nomads have often been brushed over as illiterate and unimportant, but to forget them would be a mistake, for they have left a legacy of being the great 'other' for their inclusion of women within their societies.[74]

In 1993 the body of a mummified woman was discovered preserved on an icy plateau in Siberia – so well preserved in fact, that her tattoos were still visible. The woman came to be known as the Siberian Ice Maiden, or more locally as the Ukok Princess, and revealed a lot about attitudes to women within the Pazyryk tribe she belonged to. Women were central to nomadic culture. Unlike many of the 'civilised' cultures we've already explored, women were not confined to domestic or biological functions, but in fact had higher social roles than those of men.[75] They were responsible for spiritual life, they worked with tools, and fought with weapons which were often included in their burials. Their contribution to nomadic life was necessary and their skills recognised. The burial of the Ice Maiden around 400 BCE gives us an idea of just how significant she was. As well as containing several horses (one would have been plenty to show off her status), her grave contained portable tables and altars, a silver mirror, and a last meal. But it wasn't just her horses that suggested she was someone special. Her extraordinary clothing, including a three-foot-tall headdress, was adorned with symbols of power and spirituality like the deer – a symbol of the sacred feminine which was thought to have regenerative powers and the ability to pass between this life and the next.[76] The Ice Maiden's beautifully preserved tattoos also took the shape of animals, one depicting a deer with a griffin's beak and Capricorn's antlers. All these things point to her being someone of significant status within her society; perhaps a priestess, shaman, or religious leader of some sort.[77] Although we may never know exactly who she was, the Ice Maiden was clearly very special and laid to rest accordingly by her people.

Women's status and freedoms amongst nomadic peoples were not restricted to the Pazyryk tribe. In other tribes like the Mongols, women also had more rights and freedoms than those in contemporary cultures. They shared the daily chores with men, could own and inherit property, be part of religious ceremonies, and hold religious positions. Wives of senior leaders were able to freely voice their opinions at tribal meetings and some widows and mothers even reigned as regents before a new Khan was elected as ruler.[78] Don't get me wrong, this wasn't exactly a paradise for women – over the centuries the Mongols gained a reputation for being brutal conquerors, and had a custom of abducting women from rival tribes to weaken them and strengthen their own. Women still had a predominant role in childcare and domestic duties, and polygamy was common amongst men. However, women were known to make speeches to enthuse warriors before battle; they drank, feasted, and fought alongside men, and played a vital role in the logistics of Mongol warfare.[79]

Perhaps the most famous example of the inclusion of women in Mongol society comes rather unexpectedly from Genghis Khan, who raised the status of women by putting them in positions of prominence and power. Married off to powerful tribal leaders, he installed his daughters in crucial roles administering his territories, controlling the Silk Route, and assisting in war campaigns. Following Genghis Khan's death and that of his son, women's leadership in the form of Mongol Queens became the force behind the Mongol Empire.

One such powerhouse was Khutulun, the great-great granddaughter of Genghis Khan and the last of the Mongol women to hold real power. Not much is known about the real Khutulun, but her essence has been shifted and remoulded by history into something of a mythical princess.

Born around 1260 CE at a time when the remnants of this vast empire were being squabbled over by various claimants, Khutulun was the daughter of one of the most influential of Khan's descendants. By the time Khutulun was an adult her father was the most powerful ruler in Central Asia, and she, widely respected for her battle prowess, was chosen over her brothers to be his right-hand woman. The idea that women at this time were passive, quiet, and needed to be protected never really existed. It is an edit to history. And the idea that women did not fight is also a relatively modern one. Like many Mongol women, Khutulun was not passive. She was a warrior. Throughout her childhood she trained in the three main sports of Mongolia: shooting, horse riding, and wrestling – a skill she became famed for. Whilst women in this period were no strangers to the battlefield, Khutulun was probably quite unusual for her passion and skill in wrestling. This sport was a favourite of the Mongols and an important part of courtly life. It was said that Khutulun could defeat men on the battlefield and prospective suitors in a wrestling match. Any man with designs on making her his wife was challenged to wrestle – if he couldn't best her, he gifted her horses. So skilled was Khutulun, that sources suggest she amassed a herd of thousands of horses. Eventually, she chose a husband for herself with whom she had two sons and following her father's passing continued to lead battalions on the battlefield. The death of this incredible warrior woman in 1306 put power back into the hands of men.[80]

History has feminised Khutulun, turning her from her

strong, warrior self, into some mythical, delicate wallflower sitting on the sidelines. She has been the subject of several western artistic and literary works. The famous opera *Turandot* – a story about a princess who challenges potential suitors to solve three riddles – is just one of them. In *Turandot*, suitors take up the titular character's challenge to solve her riddles and win her hand in marriage. Those who fail are executed. Turandot is presented as a cruel, icy, man-hater who needs to be conquered by love (i.e. a man) to help restore peace to the kingdom. This character is thought to be based on Khutulun and it's not hard to see the similarities; a strong woman in a position of power who has an unusual challenge for potential suitors. However, *Turandot* and other similar works depict Khutulun as a proud woman in need of saving from herself, a woman who eventually is won over by her suitor and succumbs to love. But Khutulun was not a passive fairytale princess waiting to be rescued. And whilst our idea of princesses is evolving thanks to more diverse representation from the likes of Disney, you have to wonder if modern characters like Mulan would have been possible without women like Khutulun.

Saint vs Sinner

In my second year of university, we were required to complete a study tour. This involved teaming up with four other students, choosing a historical location where we would spend two weeks conducting research, and then writing it up in a joint paper afterwards. I chose Rome.

I will never forget those two weeks. The blast of hot air as we stepped off the train at Roma Termini, the constant background hum of scooters, the intense heat of the sun on my skin. But more than all of that, the energy of the place is seared into my memory. Rome felt filled with a fizzy kind of energy – it was like being in a city that was constantly on the brink of something thrilling about to happen. The noise, the crowds, the music from street performers and the shouting of tour guides, spring flowers coming into bloom on the surrounding hills, wafts of deliciousness floating into piazzas from surrounding restaurants. It was exhilarating. Needless to say, a lot more touring than studying happened over the course of our stay. We revelled in Italian food and wine. We relished being up close with the historical monuments that, until now, we'd only ever seen in textbooks. We drank, we laughed, we had a blast. Back in the UK, we pooled our questionable notes, trawled our memories, and wrote up the paper.

Several weeks later, I was hurrying down a corridor of the Arts building on campus en route to a seminar and caught sight of the notice board where the study tour papers had been posted. I stopped to hastily check our results. A printed note from our tutor, Dr Gillian Shepherd, requested two groups come to her office to discuss their work. The black lettering jumped off the crisp white paper. My group and one other. Given the other was a group of rugby lads, my heart sank. This wasn't good.

You will perhaps be unsurprised to learn that we had spectacularly failed the module. Our paper was awful, and Dr Shepherd was unamused. I was mortified. I'd never failed anything. I'd always loved education, and my academic achievements were the thing I'd received the most praise and recognition for up until that point. I took pride in my work, always completing it to the absolute best of my ability. Perfection or bust. Failure was not an option.

I carried that core belief with me for years. Then I saw something that changed my mind. In 2016, I came across Reshma Saujani's TED Talk 'Teach girls bravery, not perfection', and it changed my whole perspective. It changed how I approached my work, how I wanted to talk to my nieces, and parent my own children; it made me realise that good enough is often exactly that – good enough. As I watched, Saujani – a lawyer, politician, and founder of the non-profit Girls Who Code – unfolded her story and bit by bit it became clear where my preoccupation with perfection might have come from. When Saujani was teaching girls to write code she made a bizarre discovery. During the first weeks of learning, students would call the tutor over and ask for help. Upon seeing their screen, the tutor would be forgiven for thinking the student had simply sat staring at a blank text editor. However, when the tutor pressed 'undo' a few times it became clear the student had tried, even come close, but ended up deleting her imperfect work. She discovered that the girls would rather present nothing at all than present something that was wrong. Perfection or bust. Saujani observed that girls in our society are frequently taught to get all A's, stay pretty, and play it safe. Boys, however, are taught to aim high, play rough, and take risks. By the time they're adults, men have learned to be brave; women to be perfect.

These days I will happily admit that I'm a recovering perfectionist. I still aim high, but I also know when to leave it at good enough. Women in ancient Rome, however, did not have such a luxury. During the late Republic and into the early Roman Empire, Roman women sat somewhere between the ancient Greeks and Egyptians in terms of status. They were citizens, but not on equal terms with men. The scant evidence we have about real women from this period is recorded almost exclusively through the lens of Rome's most elite men. Historical figures and high-profile individuals of the time like Cato and Cicero warned their fellow Romans of women's weak judgment, the risks of treating them as equals and the catastrophic consequences of women wielding any kind of influence. What we get is a clear distinction between women as either the 'ideal' – virtuous, modest, family-oriented, and kept busy with domestic work like wool weaving; or 'disreputable' – speaking out, daring to occupy public spaces, or doing scandalous work like bar tending or acting.[81] The glimpses of actual women that we do see – usually those of the highest wealth and education – give us a taste of the innovative ways women found to carve out pockets of influence and power in a man's world.

Although Roman women weren't confined to the household like in ancient Greece, their role was still considered domestic, and they had little involvement in public life. Good women were quiet women. Those who dared to speak up faced consequences. Lessons on the problem of women's voices (and the consequences of simply having one) are clear in contemporary literature like Ovid's epic *Metamorphoses*. Ovid was a poet during the beginning of the Roman Empire and his work *Metamorphoses* – a 15-book poem – is arguably his most famous and influential. The poem features several female figures who, due to their voices, present something of a problem to the men and gods in the narrative. One of these figures is the nymph Echo who is unfortunate enough to incur the wrath of the goddess Hera for her chatterbox tendencies. By keeping her in conversation, Echo prevents Hera from spying on her husband Zeus and his wandering affections. When Hera realises what Echo has been up to, she punishes her by turning Echo's voice into an instrument that simply repeats the words of others.[82] This leaves Echo unable to profess her love to Narcissus and, overcome with sadness, she wastes away until nothing is left but her voice. Another part of this epic illustrates the fate of Io, who catches the attention of the god Jupiter. When she rejects Jupiter's advances, he is enraged and uses his power to overcome and abuse her. To conceal her from his wife Juno, Jupiter turns Io into a cow. Io, now only able to moo, is left without her voice. These are just two examples. Outspoken, chatty women, or even the risk of them, were problematic. The solution? Silence.

Not only were Roman women denied a voice, but they were denied access to positions of power. Any women who managed to access power, authority, or spoke out, jarred against the accepted norm for their gender and were viewed with suspicion.[83] Happily though, not all women conformed to this man-made ideal of a quiet, wool-weaving housewife. Some broke the mould and managed to wield power and influence in their staunchly male world.

Julia Domna, the wife of Emperor Severus, used her influence to advance her position. After her husband's death, her son Caracalla placed her in a key position dealing with correspondence and responding to petitions. Formal power like this was unheard of for imperial women.[84]

Plotina, another emperor's wife and a wealthy noblewoman in her own right, used influence and ingenuity to secure her status after Emperor Trajan's death along with that of another; a young man she adored called Hadrian. Despite being less enthusiastic about Hadrian's career prospects than his wife, Trajan is said to have granted Plotina her wish and, on his death bed, named Hadrian as his successor. It's entirely possible that

Trajan did no such thing and instead, Plotina cunningly manoeuvred Hadrian's position before anyone else knew that the emperor was dead. Following his death, all Plotina had to do was voice the emperor's 'final wish'. Whatever the real version of events, Hadrian went on to have a successful reign. And Plotina? She went on to live a life of comfort, even being named as a goddess upon her death.[85]

One woman who achieved the incredible feat of creating her own power and influence without invoking the wrath of Rome's elite was Cornelia, the daughter of a famed Roman general and wife of a highly regarded senator. Cornelia was well-educated and became an intelligent presence in Roman society. After her husband's death, she chose to remain a widow – even spurning the offer of marriage from Egyptian pharaoh Ptolemy VIII. Instead, she devoted herself to raising her children and became the model Roman matron, publicly backing her sons' political careers and attempts at social reforms. Cornelia earned widespread respect and admiration for her devotion to family and state – so much so, that upon her death the city of Rome erected a statue in her honour. She became the model for future Roman women. Over the centuries, Cornelia's legacy changed and was adapted to fit society's values, over-emphasising her maternal dedication and under-egging her intellect and political influence over her sons.

But now, let me tell you about a woman who didn't just break the mould, she shattered it entirely. Around the 4th century CE, Emperor Constantine founded a new capital of the Roman Empire in the East, Constantinople. Christianity was on the rise, and the emperor was said to have converted to this new religion (although exactly how immediate and complete this conversion was is debateable). Reflecting ancient Greek ideas, Christianity polarised women into two categories. On the one hand, you had the Virgin Mary – the very definition of purity. And on the other, you had a reinterpretation of Pandora – Eve, the first woman and the root of all evil. Self-mastery was praised as a virtue, and women in Constantinople faced near-impossible standards – if you couldn't be as saintly and pure as the Virgin Mary, you must be a sinner.[86] Perfection or bust.

The arrival of Christianity brought the impossible line women were required to walk into sharper focus. The belief that sin entered the world through Eve's disobedience meant women were increasingly seen as untrustworthy.[87] Outspoken women were viewed as the source of moral pollution and once again, silence was the preferred weapon against them. This early Christian expectation of the quiet, compliant woman is captured in *The Bible, Timothy 2.11.15:*

"A woman should learn in quietness and full submission. I do not permit a woman to teach or to assume authority over a man; she must be quiet." [88]

In an environment like this, it's hard to imagine any woman asserting herself, her knowledge, or her authority without severe repercussions. Enter Theodora, the first modern woman to carve her own path to power.[89]

Unlike the previous women's stories, Theodora came from much humbler origins. Born into the lowest classes of

Byzantine society, Theodora was working as an actress, possibly also as a sex worker, when she met Justinian I – the heir to the throne. It's worth noting that the sources we have on Theodora's life before meeting Justinian are not the most reliable, the most prominent of which is regarded by historians as slanderous and based on gossip, prejudice, and second-hand accounts. As I mentioned earlier, Romans viewed women in the acting profession as disreputable and often branded them as sexually promiscuous. Translations of contemporary language used to describe women from the brothel and those on the stage have been mixed up and misaligned. It's possible that historic references to Theodora being a sex worker are in fact referencing her past work as an actress. Regardless, knowing what we do of ancient Rome's ideals, it's no surprise that marrying a woman of such a scandalous profession was against the law. However, this small matter didn't stop Theodora and Justinian. In an unprecedented move, Justinian passed a new law allowing reformed actresses to marry outside their rank. When he took the throne in 527 CE, Theodora was proclaimed empress. [90] Although never officially co-regent, Theodora used her intelligence and political acumen to transform herself into a powerful influence and her husband's most trusted advisor. Her image in mosaic at the Basilica of San Vitale shows Theodora participating in an imperial procession alongside her husband, suggesting she was seen as his intellectual and political equal.[91] This isn't hard to believe, as her name is mentioned in almost all the laws passed during Justinian's rule, and her influence is particularly evident in laws that expanded women's rights, closed brothels, and created safe houses. [92] When a plague hit

Constantinople and struck down the emperor, it was Theodora who ran state affairs while he recovered.[93] When a revolt broke out, it was Theodora who spoke out and convinced Justinian to stay and save his empire rather than flee.[94] Following the riots, they rebuilt the city with magnificent architectural testaments to their joint rule. Theodora ensured her name would never be forgotten. An inscription still exists within The Little Hagia Sophia, originally a church and now a mosque, celebrating her triumphs. She achieved the impossible. Her transformation from sinner to saint was complete.

Today, Istanbul stands where Constantinople once was. Women in modern day Turkey are fighting for the role that Theodora once had; one outside the boundaries of wife and mother, one equal to men, and one free from violence. According to the 2022 World Economic Forum's Global Gender Gap Report, out of 146 countries Turkey ranked 124th in gender equality and 112th in women's political empowerment. There is much work to do. Perhaps Theodora did manage to leave a mark though. Despite the improvements still needed to achieve gender equality, Turkish women were amongst the first in Europe to receive the right to vote and run for elected office. Today, Turkey has a strong women's movement that has contributed to the adoption of gender equality legislation and created nationwide campaigns against the widespread problem of violence against women. Brave, not perfect. I think Theodora would approve.

Fierce & fearless

When French soldiers arrived to colonise the West African Kingdom of Dahomey, they faced a force unlike anything they'd ever experienced – an army that fought with extreme discipline and valour, its soldiers full of ferocity and courage. They faced an army of women.

If you've ever seen the *Black Panther* films – a part of the Marvel Cinematic Universe, or MCU, – you may, like me, have been in awe of the women warriors who played a big part in the story. I can probably count on one hand the number of films I've watched where so many women feature in such traditionally masculine roles. To sit and watch those films was, quite frankly, refreshing.

Briefly, the story of *Black Panther* goes like this. Set in the fictional African nation of Wakanda, its people are reaping the scientific potential from a vast meteor deposit to advance technology. Led by the bloodline of tribal kings, to the outside world Wakanda appears as an underdeveloped nation with its technologies hidden away. When the true capability of Wakanda is threatened to be revealed by those determined to take the technology for themselves, war breaks out and the nation turns to the Black Panther and the Dora Milaje, Wakanda's special force of female bodyguards, for protection.

For the uninitiated, the Dora, as they are known in the film, are special indeed – particularly for a female audience who I daresay are more used to seeing white women cast as damsels in distress or 'getting the guy' at the end of the story. Bold and impactful, the main female characters within the Dora have their own opinions, agendas, and exist beyond the usual function of supporting the goals and storyline of the leading men. They are strong, independent, and take no shit. And all without a single white woman saviour in sight. In my opinion *Black Panther* showcased the power of female agency – particularly Black female agency – in a way that is rarely seen in cinema. Upon release in 2018, it was praised for having one of the most absorbing stories in the MCU along with some of the most fully realised characters.[95] So whilst I sat there enjoying the fruits of Hollywood and shovelling popcorn into my face at an embarrassing rate of knots, I was blissfully unaware that the warriors of Wakanda were based on a real army of women that existed not all that long ago. And their story is just as special.

The very much non-fictional Dahomey kingdom was established by the ancestors of the Fon people who had migrated southwards from the Niger river, settling in what is modern day Benin, West Africa. Bloody quarrels divided would-be leaders until around 1600 BCE, when three warring kingdoms emerged: Allada, Porto-Novo, and Dahomey. These kingdoms would remain at near constant war with each other, with Dahomey rising to dominance through its strategic leadership, its role in enslaving enemies from neighbouring nations, and of course the power of its army. Dahomey was reigned over by kings who were considered semi-divine and wielded supreme authority. The King controlled the social, political, and economic affairs of the Kingdom. To support him, he had a council of officials selected from the commoner class – a decision made due to the perception of commoners' loyalty and commitment.[96] Like many African societies, Fon culture was almost entirely oral with very little written down. Chroniclers of the time would recite stories in public focused on royal history, praising past and present monarchs, and very much toeing the party line. Harsh punishment, should they stray from the official narrative, was a very real possibility.[97] These stories would be replicated in bas-reliefs that decorated the palace walls at Abomey, the capital city.

Now, I appreciate that so far this is shaping up like every other patriarchy we've encountered in these pages. Powerful kings, loyal subjects, punishments for stepping out of line. However, Dahomey had a significant point of difference. One that is well worth sharing, and one that created a unique and complex experience for Dahomey's women. The culture within Dahomey was one rooted in the idea of duality and balance – similar to the ideas of balance that we explored in ancient

Egyptian and Chinese society. It is perhaps for this reason that women held a remarkably elevated status in comparison to other pre-colonial West African societies (and let's be honest, many others elsewhere too). Woven through Dahomey's political, religious, and military institutions, the idea of duality meant that all official roles from financial advisors to military generals were balanced by both male and female leaders. Women were not only able to fully participate in all aspects of life, but those belonging to the anato, or free people, were able to climb to the highest political offices. Social norms were unusually gender inclusive for a patriarchy. Girls took part in the same activities as boys and they were raised to be brave, independent, and strong. A solid basis for an army of women you might say.

Exactly when, or in fact why, this infamous band of warrior women were formed isn't clear. Often referred to as the Dahomey Amazons (a decidedly colonial reference and one I won't be using), the first recorded mention of them was in 1729. However, one of their origin stories suggests they were formed far earlier by King Huegbadja as a corp of elite elephant hunters known as the gbeto.[98] An alternative story has their beginnings as a band of royal bodyguards brought together at the request of Queen Hangbe who rose to power in the 1700s after her twin brother mysteriously died. In a patriarchal society, amassing a force of women who would give their lives to protect their queen would have been an impressive feat. Whatever their true origins, the women warriors of Dahomey reached their peak in the 19th century when they became formally integrated into Dahomey's army by King Ghezo. [99] Thanks to constant war with its neighbours, Dahomey's army was experiencing dwindling numbers of men on the battlefield and King Ghezo used this opportunity to expand the women warriors from a band of about 600 to a 6000-strong force known as the Agojie.[100] A combination of volunteers and enforced conscripts, Agojie regiments were recruited from slaves, the poor, and rebellious young girls. Only the bravest and toughest were selected and brought into the fold. The Agojie became a significant political power through their generals' place on the King's council and their access to debate important policies.

The fact that the Agojie stood apart from other African armies because of their sex is probably stating the obvious. But this wasn't the only unique thing about these warriors. The Agojie were a constant standing army. Most other nations disbanded their armies when not at war, but given Dahomey didn't exactly get on with its neighbours, the army was in a constant state of readiness. Made up of five divisions: artillery, elephant hunters, musketeers, razor women, and archers, the Agojie also wore a unique uniform that made them a highly visible and organised fighting force.[101] All Agojie warriors were renowned for their ferocity, their excellence with a rifle, and skill in hand-to-hand combat. The tactic of surprising the enemy was critical to their success and so they often used the cover of darkness in which to hide and then struck before dawn. Recruits underwent intensive training that tested their courage, endurance, and hardened them to bloodshed. One common form of training required recruits to scramble over towering walls of acacia thorns and bear the pain without complaint. The bravest received a belt made of the same thorns as a symbol of their stoicism. They also engaged in wrestling and survival training, sometimes staying out in the forest for days on end with minimal rations. In another training exercise, French Naval Officer Jean Bayol witnessed a teenage girl decapitate a condemned prisoner. He then watched as she wiped the blood from her sword and swallowed it.[102]

These women, I think you'll agree, were highly trained, savage warriors, and if you've seen *Black Panther*, you can probably appreciate where the inspiration for the Dora Milaje came from. Yet, despite their skill on the battlefield and the inclusivity of their society, it seems that the Fon people didn't view the Agojie as equals with men in any meaningful sense. This is perhaps highlighted by the fact that these women warriors were said to 'become men' at the point of their first kill.[103] This inequality is also suggested by their 'ahosi' status, meaning they were considered wives of the King and therefore subject to a certain lifestyle. This status allowed the Agojie to live in the royal palace in a female-dominated space and enjoy privileges like alcohol and tobacco. Men, with the exception of eunuchs and the King, were not permitted after sunset. I say 'wives', however I don't mean it in the literal sense. It was more of a symbolic relationship. The ahosi were considered third class wives and although they didn't sleep with the King or bear his children, they were prevented from having sex with other men. To even touch these warrior women meant certain death.[104] When the Agojie left the palace, they were preceded by a girl carrying a bell, the sound of which told every male in their path to retire to a safe distance and look the other way (something that I have to admit holds a certain appeal to me).

While women in Dahomey enjoyed significant privileges and power, their experiences were not without contradictions. They lived under the rule of a King who controlled nearly every aspect of life, yet they were free to participate in society in almost equal measure with men. Dahomey relied heavily on the slave trade, robbing people of their freedom for the Kingdom's expansion and survival, and it was the Agojie who played a significant role in capturing and selling people into slavery.

As colonialism ramped up and various European powers scrambled to absorb African countries into their empires, Dahomey now had additional enemies from which to protect itself. In 1863 King Glele, Ghezo's successor, was angered by the French declaring the neighbouring kingdom of Porto-Novo a colonial protectorate (a kingdom Glele very much considered a vassal of Dahomey). Tension between Dahomey and the European invaders increased, and war broke out. The First Franco-Dahomean War included female units of the Agojie in hand-to-hand fighting. In fact, Naval Officer Jean Bayol saw his chief gunner killed by a fighter that he recognised as the teenage girl who'd executed a prisoner in front of him just months earlier. [105] Just as many other indigenous populations experienced around the world, it was the sheer firepower of modern rifles that was Dahomey's undoing and led the French to victory.

The war that followed was fought even more fiercely than the first, with female troops in the vanguard of Dahomey's forces. The Agojie were the last to surrender, and even then, according to rumour within the French army, the survivors took their revenge by allowing themselves to be seduced by French officers. After waiting for the men to fall asleep, the women then cut the throats of their captors with their own bayonets.[106]

In 1892 the French finally seized the Dahomey capital. After the war, surviving Agojie either went into exile, served the new King – now a puppet of France – or tried to re-enter society, with varying degrees of success. The French colonisation of Dahomey proved fatal for women's rights and any privilege or power they once had was lost. The very existence of the Agojie upset French understanding of gender roles; their flaunting of ferocity, their physical power and fearlessness totally contradicted European views of how a woman should be. The colonial power brought with it a deeply Catholic culture that drew strict gender boundaries and imposed its views on a people they saw as in need of civilisation. Women were barred from political leadership and educational opportunities. European history tried hard to erase such brazen displays of female power and gender equality. As a result, the status of women in the whole region declined.

The colonial impact on Dahomey diluted the legacy of the Agojie and the relative freedom and power its women once had. As of 2024 only 26.6% of seats in Benin's parliament were held by women.[107] Whilst that may be comparable to other West African countries, consider the difference between the women who only a few hundred years prior could access the highest political offices in balance with men, and those who are living with a 50% reduction on that representation now. To have not just allowed, but actively prepared women to take the role of a warrior is highly unusual for a patriarchal society. None of the Agojie origin stories really explain why women warriors only arose in Dahomey. If we're being generous, we might put this down to the combination of gender inclusive social norms and a high degree of institutional sophistication that enabled this extraordinary army to come about. If we're being realistic, it is more likely because Dahomey was so surrounded by enemies that kings were forced to conscript women into the army to ensure the Kingdom's survival. That, and the transatlantic slave trade which contributed to women vastly outnumbering men in Dahomey's towns. We can't gloss over the reality that these women were extraordinary perpetrators of violence and regularly took part in slave raids, but nor can we allow those uncomfortable truths to stop us appreciating that when given the opportunity, these women showed that they were more than capable in a male-dominated arena. The Agojie are a reminder of what is possible.

Now, where can I get a bell?

Making progress

As a '90s child, I grew up in an era where Day-Glo colours, Alice bands, cycling shorts, and puffa jackets were all the rage. Cards on the table, I personally consider the trends of that decade to be something of a fashion blip. I did manage to avoid the dreaded shell suit; however, I vividly remember having a pair of silk tie-top blouses – one in lime green and the other bright orange – with matching Alice bands. I know, I know, I might as well have been on the runway at London Fashion Week. I do also recall having a rather fetching Day-Glo pink bum bag (or fanny pack to any American readers) that matched my sister's bright yellow one. Beautiful. The recent resurgence of '90s fashion trends has not been lost on me (although I have refused to have any part in it), and over the last few years I've noticed an increasing number of bum bag wearing individuals proudly showing off what is essentially a massive pocket. As an adult woman, I have come to appreciate the appeal of these. Having spent years lugging around a handbag – and I use the word lugging quite deliberately as I come from a long line of women who carry everything but the kitchen sink with them – my shoulders have taken a beating. Handbags are heavy and awkward; they take up the use of one hand or arm, and when you're dressed up for a night out they're a pain. Pockets, however...

...are a man thing. As much as I'd love to finish that sentence differently, for some bizarre reason fashion designers simply will not put decent pockets in women's clothing (for any designers reading this, that weird little pocket on the breast of a t-shirt does not count by the way). I find myself frequently irritated by this every time I watch my husband shove his wallet, keys, and phone neatly into his jeans pockets, whilst I can get no more than a couple of quid in the tiny, pointless pockets on mine.

As we've seen, patriarchy has always found innumerable ways to restrain women: systems of dynastic rule that passed power from father to son, imposed gender-based ideals that kept women in the home and out of politics, theories on women's inbuilt inferiority, the use of art and literature to educate society on what 'good' women looked like, and the creation of laws that literally limited women's freedoms. You know the drill by now.

Although you might have hoped that several millennia from where we started things might have moved on drastically, I'm afraid to tell you that Victorian Britain was no different. Take, for example, women's clothing with its pocketless dresses that left the wearer lumbered with 14lbs worth of corsets and underskirts that seriously restricted movement. Try doing anything radical in that. And that's the point. Women in Victorian Britain were not expected to do *anything* radical. The strict class system and gender roles meant women were expected to lead by moral example. They were to dedicate themselves to a dutiful and passive life as a wife and mother. Of course, this ideal was exactly that, an ideal. The reality of such an expectation was not possible for everybody, particularly single and working-class women who had little choice about staying put in the home and needed to take jobs like manufacturing textiles to get by. Single women were pitied and met with social disapproval. However, even the social acceptance that marriage offered came with a sacrifice. Following the wedding vows, a woman's legal status was entirely absorbed into that of her husband. [108] Married women simply didn't exist in the eyes of the law. They took their husband's name, promised to 'obey', were legally deleted and economically dependent. They became his property and responsibility with no right to sue or own property. Their wages – even their bodies – belonged to their spouse. Incredibly, it wasn't until 1992 that marital rape became illegal in the UK. Side note – an extraordinary (and quite brilliant, in my opinion) story of how one woman used this legal write-off to her advantage comes from Caroline Norton, an English social reformer who separated from her abusive husband George Norton, barrister and Member of Parliament (MP) for Guildford. After separation, she managed to sustain herself financially through work as a writer. However, her husband took her to court claiming her earnings as rightfully his because the pair were still married. No prizes for guessing who won. In retaliation, Caroline played the system and ran up enormous bills in his name. When bailiffs came knocking to claim the debts, she helpfully pointed them in her husband's direction. According to the law he was responsible for her actions and therefore her debts too. Caroline's work went on to support many women throughout the 19th century, contributing to several reforms including a woman's right to apply for custody of her children, making divorce more accessible, and allowing women to retain property post-marriage.

But back to my issue with pockets. It turns out it's not just me. There is a long history of women complaining about a lack of pockets. In an era where women had little control over anything of their own, pockets were a space controlled entirely by them, so you can kind of understand why. Now when I say space, I do in fact mean it. These pockets weren't as we know them today but rather a separate (and in some instances rather giant) tie-on accessory that would have been worn around the waist. Essentially a massive bum bag. Women carried all sorts in these pockets – in fact a contemporary advert appealing for the return of a lost or stolen one detailed the contents of one particular lady's pocket to include: a snuff box, a London almanac, an ivory carved toothpick case, silver sliding pencil, a tortoiseshell comb, a silver thimble and bodkin, keys, a red leather pocketbook, a green knit purse, five shillings, and two glass smelling bottles amongst other things.[109] This would rival the handbag contents of even my Grandma (I told you I came from a long line of handbag-fillers). Men became curious, even suspicious, about these spaces which were effectively a loophole in a system that controlled practically everything else in a woman's life. I mean, women could have who knows what in there, right?!

Towards the end of the 19th century, women had grown so sick of this shit that the beginnings of the campaign for women's suffrage – the right to vote – appeared. Change was happening, but it was slow. As is often the case, those demanding change are told they are not capable or deserving for various reasons, and when they inevitably prove that they in fact are totally capable and deserving, the people in power move the goalposts. By the turn of the century, various laws had been introduced that shifted the balance on equality, national education had a huge impact on literacy, and the White Blouse Revolution had helped women gain some economic independence as jobs like clerks, secretaries, and retail work opened up to them. Just as women gained the opportunity to prove they were equally capable as men, the goalposts were shifted. The paranoia of male-dominated unions about the new female workforce undercutting men's wages led to women struggling to challenge low wages and poor working conditions. The Marriage Bar, a restriction used in the civil service, banking, and office work that banned married women from working or applying for vacancies, meant that any woman who managed to land herself a decent job had to give it all up as soon as she said 'I do'. Armed with a better education, improved literacy, and determination for change, the way was paved for women in Britain to campaign for the vote.

Thankfully, despite a landscape where radical acts were unbecoming of the ideal woman, radical women did exist. I'm risking being rather reductive here, but the campaign for women's suffrage was long, complex, and ultimately splintered into two dominating groups: the suffragists led by Millicent Fawcett, and the suffragettes led by Emmeline Pankhurst, with many others in between. Both these powerhouses of activism chose wildly different methods to get their message across. The largest women's rights association, Fawcett's National Union of Women's Suffrage Societies (NUWSS), led a campaign that was law-abiding and democratic, aiming to achieve its goals through introducing Parliamentary Bills. In contrast, Pankhurst's Women's Social and Political Union (WSPU) developed a strategy that challenged the core expectations of women's behaviour. They chose to dispense with words, petitions, and patient lobbying in favour of a militant campaign that couldn't be ignored. By committing violent acts like breaking windows, defacing artwork, and setting fire to post boxes, the suffragettes ensured they were heard, but risked prison sentences, hunger strikes, and the horror of forced feeding.

All these incredible women confronted and challenged traditional ideas of femininity and respectability. And for that they were subject to intense criticism. They came under fire for everything from their clothing to the neglect of their family. I continue to find it fascinating that women who drive for change are seen as aggressive, self-serving shrews, yet when men do it, they are visionary radicals. Artwork of this period – both pro- and anti-suffrage – shows just how concerned society still was with the 'proper' place of women. Anti-suffrage propaganda focused on images of broken or dysfunctional homes; one such poster – *A Suffragettes Home* – featured a husband returning home to crying, neglected children, whilst his wife is out at a suffragette meeting. Others depicted reversed gender roles (perish the thought). Men who supported the feminist cause were openly ridiculed and endured slurs on their masculinity, whilst women were depicted as unnatural, manly, and unattractive. Same stuff, different century. On the pro side, images showed women's ability to perform their domestic roles *and* simultaneously take part in politics, all the while stressing their femininity and womanhood. This expression of femininity was important in asserting their desire – and right – to exist in public as women, not men.

It was around this time that these massive tie-on pockets started disappearing. The suspicious accessory had become associated with the suffrage movement, which suddenly meant that those who had them were seen as improper, shady, or masculine in some way. Dress became an important weapon of the suffrage movement. Women were keenly aware of the propaganda challenging their femininity, and the suffragettes in particular took care to dress in conventional clothes that defined them as womanly so as not to give the press or anti-suffrage voices even more ammunition against them.

The outbreak of war in Europe brought further change for women. Despite initially pausing the campaign for the vote, it became an enormous accelerating force upon women's suffrage and equality. A society that had feared giving women the vote would remove them from their proper place (and according to Lord Curzon – a prominent British statesman and politician – lead to the weakening of Britain) suddenly had no choice about bringing women into the public sphere. Women of all classes were needed for the war effort. This was an opportunity to challenge those stubborn and outdated perceptions and demonstrate their physical and mental capabilities in the workplace on a scale never seen before. It still didn't stop the patriarchy finding more ways to control the gains women had made. In 1917 women's clothing would cause problems again when two female employees were fired from the Metallurgical Company in Newcastle for daring to wear trousers outside the factory gates.[110] Yes, trousers. When the rest of their female colleagues at the factory stopped work until they were reinstated, all of them were dismissed. It turns out that as a woman in 1917 you could go after men's jobs, but going after their clothing was a bridge too far. Goalposts moved.

Finally, in 1918, women won the vote. But political and societal fear prevented it from being on the same terms as men. Virtually all men over the age of 21 could vote, whereas women had to be over the age of 30 and have some manner of wealth to qualify. The rest would have to wait another decade. Post war, fear dominated attitudes towards women's place in society. The population was now majority female due to having lost so many men which, had women received the vote on equal terms, would have given them a majority in the British electorate. Nobody knew how women would vote, and that scared the politicians. Concerns about low birth rates scared society, and that meant women were required to get back to their childbearing duties. Pay packets that had given women independence and the ability to earn, spend, and play like men suddenly felt threatening to the returning jobless war veterans.

Despite this familiar 'two steps forward, one step back'

feel to the progress of women's equality, in 1919 Nancy Astor made history and became the first woman to take her seat in Parliament. Early women MPs focused on influencing laws and championing reforms in healthcare, family allowance, divorce laws, and the guardianship of children – topics that were perceived to be 'women's issues'. Whilst these topics were incredibly important to address and made a huge difference to women's autonomy, this (in my opinion) rather unhelpful branding continued the effort to put women and their contributions in a box with a big shiny label that read 'DOMESTIC'. Women could have their politics as long as they stayed in their lane. But it was the beginning of a change that couldn't be halted.

In 1928 women in Britain finally received the right to vote on equal terms with men. In the decades that followed this massive leap forward, women continued the fight to remove other barriers to equality and level the playing field – to gain access to the same opportunities, equal treatment, and have their voices equally valued. It's been around 100 years since that hard-won achievement. In the last century there has been further progress still, but I think you'd be amazed at how late some of the rights we perhaps take for granted were enshrined in law. Here's a (very) quick rundown of just some of the milestones reached in the last century in Britain.

Inter-war period

After so many years focused on women's suffrage, the feminist movement divides and different groups focus on a range of issues, from those that specifically impact women to campaigning for no distinction in law between the sexes. Some fight against the age old 'fragile female' notion and campaign to remove protectionist legislation that prevented women working certain jobs deemed too dangerous. (Yes, seriously. Women could not, for example, work with lead paint as it was viewed as too dangerous for our delicate constitutions. Obviously with what we now know when it comes to lead paint, we all have delicate constitutions! But the point remains valid.)

Post-war Britain

Dorothy Evans – previously a suffragette and later in life an equal rights campaigner – works to introduce the Equal Citizenship Bill which would eradicate gender discrimination in British law. Rather than fighting to amend over 30 laws that discriminated between men and women, she campaigns for one blanket bill. However, she died suddenly in 1944 and with her death momentum is lost and the bill forgotten.

1950s

Women are entitled to sit in the House of Lords for the first time.

1960s

Second-wave Feminism broadens the equality debate by addressing issues beyond legal barriers and by targeting domestic violence, sexuality, and reproductive rights, striving to include a diversity of voices.

The contraceptive pill becomes available on the National Health Service.

The 1967 Abortion Act gives women in the UK (excluding Northern Ireland) abortion rights under certain conditions.

Radical figures like Germaine Greer challenge ideas of women's inferiority and their natural dependence on men. Sheila Rowbotham writes about how the patriarchy has undermined women's rights.

Jayaben Desai begins one of the longest strikes in British history in an effort to improve her working conditions. It is the first strike where ethnic minority workers receive proper support from Trade Unions.

Men increasingly begin showing support for women's equality.

1970s

In 1975 – 30 years after Dorothy Evans tried to pass the Equal Citizenship Bill – the Sex Discrimination Act comes in, protecting men and women from discrimination on the basis of sex in areas like the purchase of goods, education, and employment.

Women are able to have their own bank accounts independent of their husbands for the first time and apply for loans or credit in their own name.

The first women's refuge is set up in Chiswick by Erin Prizzy.

The Equal Pay Act is created off the back of the Ford Dagenham sewing machinist's strike and seeks to stop unfavourable treatment in pay and conditions of employment. It is superseded 40 years later by the Equality Act in 2010.

The end of the decade sees Britain elect its first female Prime Minister – Margaret Thatcher.

1980s

If you can believe it, it isn't until 1982 that women can finally buy a pint down the pub without being refused service.[111]

Diane Abbot becomes the first Black female MP.

Legislation dealing with violence against women criminalises Female Genital Mutilation.

Statutory Maternity Pay is introduced in 1986.

1990s

Milestones around family and marriage begin to be reached.

Statutory Maternity Pay is quickly followed by Statutory Maternity Leave.

Rape in marriage is criminalised.

Under sex discrimination regulations, it becomes illegal for employers to discriminate against trans people.

2000s

In 2002, Parliament passes measures to allow gay, lesbian, and unmarried couples to adopt children.

Domestic violence is tackled by making common assault an arrestable offence.

Fathers become entitled to two week's paid paternity leave.

2010s

The Equality Act in 2010 simplifies, updates, and brings together laws dealing with discrimination on the basis of sex, race, disability, pay, religion or belief, age, and sexual orientation.

In 2014 shared parental leave is introduced and same-sex marriage is finally legalised.[112]

Coercive control becomes a criminal offence.

Abortion in Northern Ireland is legalised.

Upskirting – where someone takes a picture under a person's clothing (for example, a skirt) without them knowing – becomes a criminal offence under the Voyeurism Act.

The first female statue is placed in Parliament Square – it is a statue of Millicent Fawcett.

2020s

The 2021 Domestic Abuse Act defines domestic abuse and extends protections for victims post-separation from their abusive partner.

In October 2021, the 'Girls Night In' protest sees women across the UK boycott bars and nightclubs to highlight the problem of drink spiking and spiking by needle. In 2024, the King's Speech announces government plans to introduce a new law to make spiking a specific offence.

Women's football is catapulted into the spotlight when the Lionesses (the England women's football team) win the 2022 UEFA Women's Championship. They follow that by getting to the final of the 2023 World Cup. The BBC's coverage of that final is watched by 21.2 million people.[113]

As this brings us almost up to present day, it's important to appreciate just how far we've come in progressing attitudes towards women, equality, and beginning the process of removing age-old stereotypes and a system geared towards men. Many of us have probably never questioned our right to an education, to open a bank account, own our own property, or get served in a pub. But these were hard-won rights – rights that still don't exist for women in many parts of the world today.

Even with the incredible milestones reached in the UK over the last century, there are still many remaining barriers to equality: women still make up less than half of MPs, we are still judged by what we wear and how we look, perceptions of 'proper' behaviours expected of us creates biases when we don't conform, and we still endure gender-based abuse in public.

Where does that leave us? In a better place certainly, but still with a lot of work to do. Also, much to my irritation, still pocketless. So, the next time you hear a woman moaning about a lack of pockets in her clothing, tell her that you understand. It's not just about the pocket.

Parting Thoughts: Reclaiming Our Story

"Honestly the best marketing scheme in history is men successfully getting away with calling women the "more emotional" gender for like, EONS, because they've successfully rebranded anger as Not An Emotion."

Claire Willett, playwright & author

I remember seeing the *Mona Lisa* for the first time and being wildly underwhelmed. I hadn't expected her to be so tiny. I also remember being confused about all the fuss with her smile (or her lack of it depending on your view). It reminded me of the expression a woman makes when a man has just told her to "smile, love". Polite compliance mixed with mild irritation. *What was the big deal?* That particular time spent in Paris was a small part of a much bigger backpacking tour of Europe I was doing that summer. The *Mona Lisa* was a tiny fragment of a chaotic few weeks. A fleeting memory amongst a myriad of others. Seen and then instantly forgotten, just as history has treated many of the women we've met in this book. The irony.

Fast forward years later and I'm back in Paris and once again stood in front of that enigmatic portrait. This time though I understood what I was looking at. Much time has been spent by experts studying her; speculating on who she was, why Leonardo Da Vinci chose to capture her in the way he did, and why her smile seems to be there one minute and not the next. Art experts will tell you that Da Vinci's technique of using irregular brushstrokes, merging paint instead of using outlines, and seamlessly blending light to dark makes her more realistic, more alive. They will tell you that his choices of pose, background, and perspective all deviated from the traditional portraiture of the period making her unusual, special, priceless. All of that is true. But for me, that isn't why she's so captivating. That isn't why her mystique keeps millions of visitors flocking to her home at the Louvre every year. I think Da Vinci captured a real woman just as the world was meant to see her. *Mona Lisa* does not conform to society's expectations. She does not strive to be portrayed like the Italian nobility of the time, showing off her social status through fancy clothes and flamboyant hairstyles. She doesn't smile because a man has told her to. You might be fooled into thinking that her expression represents a woman who is passive and demure. Unlike typical female portraiture of the era, she meets our gaze directly, just as a man would. That 'Mona Lisa smile' is not passive and demure. It is knowing. She smiles because she knows our secret. She knows what women are worth. And she knows the world is yet to understand. She has always been right in front of us, and yet she has never been truly seen. Her story has been told a thousand different ways. Her image has been stolen and exploited by those trying to teach the world a lesson. She is women everywhere.

And so here we are, stroll through history complete and we're left with that question; why are things the way they are? Why do girls and women grow up believing that brilliance belongs to the boys?

Because from the very beginnings of what history

recognises as civilisation, we've been lied to. We've been told lies about our potential and our capability. About our intelligence and our bodies. About what it means to be 'good' and what will happen if we're not. Just as historic legends and myths warned what would become of the wayward woman – the woman who spoke up or ventured out – our own childhood stories belie the dangers of wandering too far from the expected path, with promises of being eaten by big bad wolves or cast out from society. Erasure or villainy; the price you pay for daring to stray. If you believed the version of history that most of us have been taught, you might believe that women are weak, hysterical misfits in need of constant male protection and guidance. You might believe that good women are quiet, passive, and stay in their lane. You might believe that women are of most use kept tucked away at home where we can do what we do best – make babies and keep husbands happy. No need for ambition or dreams, ladies. Much better to leave the stuff that society really values to the men – the politics, the leadership, the military clout, the intellectual prowess. But we know different. Whether by default or defiance, we've met women within these pages who have risen beyond the fallacies we've been told to become rulers, warriors, and scholars. They have proved time and again their capability as leaders, storytellers, creators, and lawmakers. Women's capability, or should I say lack of it, is a myth. One that has been borne of the historical sweeping under the carpet of female success and the distorted yardstick against which we are measured. Over millennia we have been tamed, caged, and othered. And why? To ensure that those in power retain it. *History isn't what happened. It's who tells the story.*

For thousands of years women have been relegated to the status of the second citizen. And we are still carrying this ancient baggage. Baggage that includes wildly incorrect ideas about the female body. Baggage that requires us to prove ourselves over and over again. Baggage that includes restrictive gender roles designed to suit those in power. And this baggage is heavy, it weighs us down. We have to wade daily through the biases, stereotypes, and beliefs about us that it has created. It is these very same hand-me-down ideas that mean even in the 21st century women who take control of their own lives and pursue their own dreams are seen as selfish and difficult. It is these ideas that mean women are presumed to be the carers of children or elderly relatives. It is these ideas that mean women who display any kind of emotion are labelled hysterical. And it is these ideas that mean any women in power are viewed with suspicion.

We're done carrying these bags.

So how do we change the way it is? That's a big question. And one where I think it's easy to get drawn into creating a fix for women: lessons on how to be assertive and lead more 'like a man', gender quotas for MPs, coaching and mentoring programmes aimed at boosting women's skill sets, or initiatives to encourage girls into traditionally male-dominated careers. None of these are bad ideas; in fact, there is evidence to show that they work. But if we're not careful they risk missing the point. Women do not need 'fixing' because women are not the problem. The problem is the system. It is the societal structures that have kept the fallacies about us alive for centuries, that were designed to keep power in male hands, and that have taught us all to prize and prioritise men and their contributions. It is the patriarchal system that has kept women quiet, out of positions of authority, and doubting ourselves. It is the system that has ignored, distorted, or omitted from the history books women's contributions with such frequency that we have been fooled into believing this is just the way it is. And whilst this all sounds absolutely ideal for men (and largely, it is), it's important to note that it is this same system that has weaponised masculinity, made it toxic, and thrown it back at men having them believe that without their inherited power and dominance over others they are somehow 'less than'. The system hurts us all. Any fixes that we offer, therefore, have to go hand in hand with educating the world about the lies we have been told and the possibilities that open up if we choose to leave this narrative behind.

And when it comes to dismantling the myth that brilliance belongs to the boys? There is hope. We learned all this. And if we learned it, we can unlearn it too. For too long those in power have told our story. The wrong story. We've had it dissected, rearranged, and retold to us in such a way that it is unrecognisable from the one the world was meant to hear. Women are not biologically and mentally inferior, weak, or prone to wandering uteruses. Far from it. Women are powerful and capable. It's time to take our narrative back. It is time that we start sharing women's stories and our lost histories. It is time that we tell our story as it was always meant to be – that women were the first artists and authors; that females hunted and fought; that women ruled civilisations, built entire cities, influenced empires, and created peace and stability; that women's voices should not be ignored.

In the 10 years since I first took that dive into my beliefs and expectations of what success looks like for me as a woman, I have learned a lot. I now understand where some of those expectations came from, how the subtle (and not so subtle) messages handed down from history had shaped my thinking. I now understand why certain career paths never crossed my mind and why I subconsciously held marriage and children as milestones of success. I now understand more than ever that there is another side to the history I had been taught and what we women are battling against. I am now ready. Ready to redefine success on my own terms and reject a system designed to keep us all quiet and in our lane. I am ready to say to our collective baggage, "No thanks. I want to be heard, to take up space, to grab opportunities to grow and add value; to aim for my own definition of success. I am a square peg in a round hole. But I refuse to let my corners be sanded down to fit a society that was not designed for me. I'd rather reshape the hole."

If you take anything from these pages, please let it be this:

Define success for yourself: forget societal expectations and go after what you believe in. You are capable of greatness.

Share women's true history: women have a beautiful history full of bravery, battles, and brilliance. Tell the world.

Be your brilliant self: always.

Our journey through history has shown that women have far too much to offer to allow parts of us to be sanded down and lost. The world has been allowed to forget who we are and what we can do.

It's time to remind it.

ACKNOWLEDGEMENTS

The very reason this book even exists at all is down to these people here – to you all, I am forever grateful:

Richard – my husband, best friend, rock, and biggest cheerleader. Thank you for your unwavering support and understanding. You have helped me carve out the hundreds of hours this has taken, without question or complaint. I love you.

Dave – my personal writing guru. A huge thank you for your time, guidance, and mentorship. It has been a privilege to learn from you. Those pub lunches have been a huge help along to way too!

Jess – for taking the time to proof-read my work and spot the mistakes I'd missed.

To my many friends and colleagues who have shown interest, encouragement, and support. You have stoked my self-belief when I questioned it.

To my history teacher at college, Shaun, who set me down this path all those years ago. Thank you. I suspect you will never know what you set in motion. And to all those lecturers at the University of Birmingham who poured such passion into their teaching – please know that you left a bit of that with me.

To all the incredible authors whose work I have read but who I have never met – Caroline Criado Perez, Amanda Foreman, Laura Bates, Glennon Doyle, Elizabeth Lesser, Helen Lewis, and many,

many others – thank you for your words, your inspiration, and your activism. You are forging paths that allow others like me to follow. The world needs you. Please know you make a difference.

Finally, to my parents. Thank you for the education and opportunities you gave me, and for raising me to go after what I believe in. I hope I can make even just a small impact on the girls and women reading this and inspire them to go after what they believe in too.

About the Author

Kerry Laker-Fry is a writer, coach, and advocate for women's empowerment and equality. With a degree in Ancient History and Archaeology from the University of Birmingham, she has long been fascinated by the stories of the past, the ones that society chooses to tell—and more importantly, the ones it leaves out.

A passionate storyteller, Kerry's writing seeks to challenge the narratives that have historically sidelined women. She has published articles with *The F Word* and *WomenBeing* magazine, taking the opportunity to shine a light on women's stories and contemporary feminist issues.

In her work as an Organisational Development Partner, Kerry helps others unlock their personal and professional growth. Guided by her philosophy 'I can do anything, but not everything' she looks to challenge thinking and inspire action, one conversation at a time. To help achieve this, she founded SHE: The Success Coach, a company dedicated to helping women develop the confidence, capability, and voice they need to succeed.

When she's not unearthing forgotten female brilliance, Kerry is a keen adventurer, lifelong learner, parent, and a firm believer that history—and success—shouldn't be a boy thing.

REFERENCES

REFERENCES

---

[1] Sigmund Freud, 'Femininity', *New Introductory Lectures on Psychoanalysis*, in *The Standard Edition (vol. 22)*, 113

[2] https://www.forbes.com/lists/innovative-leaders/#1786817926aa

[3] 'Gender stereotypes about intellectual ability emerge early and influence children's interests' by Lian Bian, Sarah-Jane Leslie & Andrei Cimpian' cited in 'Science' 27 Jan 2017: Vol. 355, Issue 6323, pp. 389-391

[4] The Guardian article 'Girls believe brilliance is a male trait, research into gender stereotypes shows' by Nicola Davis, 2017

[5] https://www.alternet.org/2013/09/most-depressing-discovery-about-brain-ever/

[6] National Geographic 'Prehistoric female hunter discovery upends gender role assumptions' by Maya Wei-Haas, 2020

[7] National Geographic 'Were the first artists mostly women?' by Virginia Hughes, 2013 https://www.nationalgeographic.com/adventure/article/131008-women-handprints-oldest-neolithic-cave-art

[8] National Geographic 'Were the first artists mostly women?' by Virginia Hughes, 2013 https://www.nationalgeographic.com/adventure/article/131008-women-handprints-oldest-neolithic-cave-art

[9] https://www.nationalgeographic.com/history/magazine/2019/03-04/early-agricultural-settlement-catalhoyuk-turkey/

10

https://www.bbc.co.uk/programmes/articles/1dRznJkKZ6DnG0fXMD2hxNP/catalhoyuk-an-example-of-true-gender-equality

---

[11] https://www.bbc.co.uk/programmes/articles/1dRznJkKZ6DnG0fXMD2hxNP/catalhoyuk-an-example-of-true-gender-equality

[12] https://www.mindtools.com/a4denhh/maslows-hierarchy-of-needs

[13] https://www.bbc.co.uk/programmes/articles/4vD023dn4cp8wF2lRntcQ7L/is-gender-inequality-man-made

[14] 'Women's Writing of ancient Mesopotamia' by Charles Halton & Saana Svard, 2017 chpt. 2

[15] 'Ascent of Woman: Civilisations' television series, by Dr Amanda Foreman

[16] 'Ascent of Woman: Civilisations' television series, by Dr Amanda Foreman

[17] 'A History of the Ancient Near East' by Marc Van De Mieroop, 2004 pgs. 53-54

[18] https://www.worldbank.org/en/news/press-release/2022/03/01/nearly-2-4-billion-women-globally-don-t-have-same-economic-rights-as-men

[19] 'Women's Writing of ancient Mesopotamia' by Charles Halton & Saana Svard, 2017 chpt. 2

[20] 'Women's Writing of ancient Mesopotamia' by Charles Halton & Saana Svard, 2017 chpt. 2

[21] 'Ancient Iraq' by Georges Roux, 1992, pgs. 87-91

[22] 'Ancient Iraq' by Georges Roux, 1992, pg. 85

[23] 'Ascent of Woman: Civilisations' television series, by Dr Amanda Foreman

[24] 'Ancient Iraq' by Georges Roux, 1992, pg. 203

[25] 'Ascent of Woman: Civilisations' television series, by Dr Amanda Foreman

[26] 'A History of the Ancient Near East' by Marc Van De Mieroop, 2004 pgs. 173-174

[27] 'A History of the Ancient Near East' by Marc Van De Mieroop, 2004 pg. 174

[28] 'A History of the Ancient Near East' by Marc Van De Mieroop, 2004 pgs. 173-174

[29] 'Ascent of Woman: Civilisations' television series, by Dr Amanda Foreman

[30] Ancient History Encyclopaedia – 'Women in Ancient Egypt' by Joshua J. Mark 2016

[31] BBC History 'From Warrior Women to Female Pharaohs: Careers for Women in Ancient Egypt' by Joann Fletcher, 2011

[32] 'Dancing for Hathor: Women in Ancient Egypt' by Carolyn Garves-Brown, 2010 pg. 2

[33] Ancient History Encyclopaedia – 'Women in Ancient Egypt' by Joshua J. Mark 2016

[34] National Geographic 'The truth behind Egypt's female pharaohs and their power' by Simon Worrall, 2018

[35] TEDx Talk 'The Athena Doctrine', John Gerzema, 2012

[36] 'The Oxford History of Ancient Egypt' by Ian Shaw, 2000 pg. 171

[37] 'Hatshepsut' by Joyce Tyldesley, 1996 pg.18

[38] National Geographic 'The King Herself' by Chip Brown 2009

---

[39] National Geographic 'The King Herself' by Chip Brown 2009

[40] National Geographic 'The truth behind Egypt's female pharaohs and their power' by Simon Worrall, 2018

[41] National Geographic 'The King Herself' by Chip Brown 2009

[42] 'Hatchepsut: The Female Pharaoh' by Joyce Tyldesley, 1996 pg.225

[43] 'Hatchepsut: The Female Pharaoh' by Joyce Tyldesley, 1996 pg.226-227

[44] 'Hatchepsut: The Female Pharaoh' by Joyce Tyldesley, 1996 pg.230

[45] 'Ascent of Woman: Civilisations' television series, by Dr Amanda Foreman

[46] Lun Yu collection, Chapter XVII cited in Gao, Xiongya. "Women Existing for Men: Confucianism and Social Injustice against Women in China." *Race, Gender & Class* 10, no. 3 (2003): 114-25. Accessed August 12, 2020. www.jstor.org/stable/41675091

[47] 'Ascent of Woman: Civilisations' television series, by Dr Amanda Foreman

[48] Gao, Xiongya. "Women Existing for Men: Confucianism and Social Injustice against Women in China." *Race, Gender & Class* 10, no. 3 (2003): 114-25. Accessed August 12, 2020. www.jstor.org/stable/41675091

[49] https://www.britannica.com/biography/Dong-Zhongshu

[50] Wang, Robin R. "Dong Zhongshu's Transformation of 'Yin-Yang' Theory and Contesting of Gender Identity." Philosophy East and West 55, no. 2 (2005): 209–31. http://www.jstor.org/stable/4487951.

[51] 'Ascent of Woman: Civilisations' television series, by Dr Amanda Foreman

---

[52] Gao, Xiongya. "Women Existing for Men: Confucianism and Social Injustice against Women in China." *Race, Gender & Class* 10, no. 3 (2003): 114-25. Accessed August 12, 2020. www.jstor.org/stable/41675091 pg. 118

[53] Gao, Xiongya. "Women Existing for Men: Confucianism and Social Injustice against Women in China." *Race, Gender & Class* 10, no. 3 (2003): 114-25. Accessed August 12, 2020. www.jstor.org/stable/41675091 pg. 121

[54] Gao, Xiongya. "Women Existing for Men: Confucianism and Social Injustice against Women in China." *Race, Gender & Class* 10, no. 3 (2003): 114-25. Accessed August 12, 2020. www.jstor.org/stable/41675091 pg. 118

[55] Gao, Xiongya. "Women Existing for Men: Confucianism and Social Injustice against Women in China." *Race, Gender & Class* 10, no. 3 (2003): 114-25. Accessed August 12, 2020. www.jstor.org/stable/41675091

[56] 'Images of Women in Chinese Thought & Culture: Writings from the Pre-Qin Period Through the Song Dynasty', by Robin Wang, 2003, pg. 328

[57] 'Ascent of Woman: Civilisations' television series, by Dr Amanda Foreman

[58] The New York Times, 'Young Chinese Women Are Defying the Communist Party', by Leta Hong Fincher, 26th November 2023

[59] The New York Times, 'China's Male Leaders Signal to Women That Their Place Is in the Home', by Alexandra Stevenson, 2nd November 2023

[60] 'Ascent of Woman: Civilisations' television series, by Dr Amanda Foreman

[61] Smithsonian Magazine article 'The Demonization of Empress Wu' by Mike Dash, 2012

[62] 'Ascent of Woman: Civilisations' television series, by Dr Amanda Foreman

---

[63] Smithsonian Magazine article 'The Demonization of Empress Wu' by Mike Dash, 2012

[64] Smithsonian Magazine article 'The Demonization of Empress Wu' by Mike Dash, 2012

[65] https://dictionary.cambridge.org/dictionary/english/civilized

[66] 'Ascent of Woman: Civilisations' television series, by Dr Amanda Foreman

[67] 'The Cambridge Companion to Ancient Greek Law' by Michael Gagarin & David Cohen, 2005, pg. 238

[68] 'Ascent of Woman: Civilisations' television series, by Dr Amanda Foreman

[69] 'The Cambridge Companion to Ancient Greek Law' by Michael Gagarin & David Cohen, 2005, pg. 238

[70] Quote from Euripides's 'Medea' in 'Euripides: Ten Plays' by Paul Roche, 1998, pg. 345

[71] 'The Cambridge Companion to Ancient Greek Law' by Michael Gagarin & David Cohen, 2005, pg. 250

[72] 'The Cambridge Companion to Ancient Greek Law' by Michael Gagarin & David Cohen, 2005, pg. 245

[73] 'The Cambridge Companion to Ancient Greek Law' by Michael Gagarin & David Cohen, 2005, pgs. 252-253

[74] 'Ascent of Woman: Civilisations' television series, by Dr Amanda Foreman

[75] 'Ascent of Woman: Civilisations' television series, by Dr Amanda Foreman

---

[76] 'Ascent of Woman: Civilisations' television series, by Dr Amanda Foreman

[77] The Siberian Times article 'Iconic 2,500 year old Siberian princess 'died from breast cancer', reveals MRI scan' by Anna Liesowska, 2014

[78] Ancient History Encyclopaedia 'Women in the Mongol Empire' by Mark Cartwright, 2019

[79] Ancient History Encyclopaedia 'Women in the Mongol Empire' by Mark Cartwright, 2019

[80] https://en.wikipedia.org/wiki/The_Secret_History_of_the_Mongol_Queens

[81] BBC History website 'Roman Women: Following the Clues' by Suzanne Dixon, 2011

[82] 'Women & Power: A Manifesto' by Mary Beard, 2017

[83] 'Women in Ancient Societies' by Susan Fischler, 1994, pg. 116

[84] Time article 'Women in Ancient Rome Didn't Have Equal Rights. They Still Changed History' by Barry Strauss, 2019

[85] Time article 'Women in Ancient Rome Didn't Have Equal Rights. They Still Changed History' by Barry Strauss, 2019

[86] 'Ascent of Woman: Civilisations' television series, by Dr Amanda Foreman

[87] Ancient History Encyclopaedia – 'Women in Ancient Egypt' by Joshua J. Mark 2016

[88] https://www.bible.com/bible/111/1TI.2.11-15.NIV

[89] 'Ascent of Woman: Civilisations' television series, by Dr Amanda Foreman

---

[90] https://www.britannica.com/biography/Theodora-Byzantine-empress-died-548

[91] https://www.brooklynmuseum.org/eascfa/dinner_party/place_settings/theodora

[92] https://www.brooklynmuseum.org/eascfa/dinner_party/place_settings/theodora

[93] 'Ascent of Woman: Civilisations' television series, by Dr Amanda Foreman

[94] https://www.britannica.com/biography/Theodora-Byzantine-empress-died-548

[95] https://www.rottentomatoes.com/m/black_panther_2018

[96] National Geographic article 'The warriors of this West African kingdom were formidable—and female' by Rachel Jones, 2022

[97] https://www.getty.edu/conservation/publications_resources/pdf_publications/pdf/palace2.pdf

[98] Smithsonian Magazine article 'Dahomey's Women Warriors' by Mike Dash, 2011

[99] National Geographic article 'The warriors of this West African kingdom were formidable—and female' by Rachel Jones, 2022

[100] Smithsonian Magazine article 'The Real Warriors Behind 'The Woman King' by Meilan Solly, 2022

[101] Smithsonian Magazine article 'The Real Warriors Behind 'The Woman King' by Meilan Solly, 2022

[102] Smithsonian Magazine article 'Dahomey's Women Warriors' by Mike Dash, 2011

---

[103] Smithsonian Magazine article 'Dahomey's Women Warriors' by Mike Dash, 2011

[104] Smithsonian Magazine article 'Dahomey's Women Warriors' by Mike Dash, 2011

[105] Smithsonian Magazine article 'Dahomey's Women Warriors' by Mike Dash, 2011

[106] Smithsonian Magazine article 'Dahomey's Women Warriors' by Mike Dash, 2011

107

https://data.unwomen.org/country/benin#:~:text=Globally%2C%20some%20progress%20on%20women's,94%20per%201%2C000%20in%202014.

[108] 'A Brief Summary, in Plain Language, of the Most Important Laws of England Concerning Women: Together With a Few Observations Thereon' By Barbara Leigh Smith Bodichon, 1869, pg. 9

[109] Visible Women podcast with Caroline Criado Perez, Episode 5. 'The curious case of Percy Pig and the missing pocket', July 2022

[110] 'Difficult Women' by Helen Lewis, 2020, pg. 105

[111] The Guardian article 'Women's rights and their money: a timeline from Cleopatra to Lilly Ledbetter' by Suzanne McGee & Heidi Moore, 2014

[112] Fawcett Society report '150 years of progress on women's rights and gender equality 1866-2016'

113

https://www.bbc.co.uk/sport/football/66567881#:~:text=The%20Women's%20World%20Cup%20final,television%20coverage%20of%20the%20tournament.

Printed in Great Britain
by Amazon

62026736R00078